Seva

Seva

Sikh Wisdom for Living Well
by Doing Good

Jasreen Mayal Khanna

SOUVENIR
PRESS

First published in Great Britain in 2022 by
Souvenir Press,
an imprint of Profile Books Ltd
29 Cloth Fair
London
EC1A 7JQ
www.souvenirpress.co.uk

First published in India in 2021 by Juggernaut Books

Typeset in Adobe Caslon Pro by R. Ajith Kumar, Noida

1 3 5 7 9 10 8 6 4 2

Printed and bound in Great Britain by
Clays Ltd, Elcograf S.p.A.

A CIP catalogue record for this book is available from the British Library.

ISBN 978 1 800810 07 5
eISBN 978 1 782839 66 8

FSC
www.fsc.org
MIX
Paper from
responsible sources
FSC® C018072

For my parents, Shaji and Simmy
Thank you for giving me wings

Contents

Preface

I wrote this book to celebrate everything I love about Sikhism. I am a Sikh because I was born into a Sikh family but I also genuinely enjoy being part of this community, believing that it makes me a happier and more joyful person. I think all people, religious or not, can benefit from the way we approach life.

You've probably seen Sikh men with their distinctive beards and turbans or have spotted our gurdwaras (Sikh temples) which serve free food to all, or maybe you've heard Sikh holy chants, called kirtans, while doing a Kundalini yoga class. But who are the Sikhs? What is seva? And what drives our fearless generosity in helping absolute strangers? Let me give you some background before I deliver lessons derived from our culture and faith.

Sikhism, or Sikhi, is the youngest world religion at 552 years old. It has about 30 million followers; 22 million reside in India and the rest abroad – they're considered a thriving and prosperous expat community world over from Birmingham, UK to Vancouver, Canada. We call our men sardars and women sardarnis. Our gurdwaras aren't just temples, they're also soup kitchens and homeless shelters. When we visit, we first bow our head down to our holy book called the Guru Granth Sahib, then pray and listen to soulful kirtans and eventually make our way to the kitchen area. There we all help to cook a simple, tasty meal called langar which is served for free to anyone who wishes to partake in it. We do all this because it is part of our culture but to fully understand Sikhi we need to look at the context in which it was created.

The founder of Sikhism, Guru Nanak was born in the fifteenth century when the society in erstwhile Punjab (the original land of the Sikhs, and now a state in India bordering Pakistan) was rather unequal. The Hindu caste system was prevalent among the masses and the land was ruled the by Mughal monarchy. Nanak's solution to this was to preach about kindness, equality and hard work and to tell his disciples to incorporate these values into their daily lives. His revolutionary idea was to help others without any expectation of reward or personal gain in return. This is how seva – or 'selfless service' – was born and it is the most impactful thing the Sikh community does. Hence it is the topic and title of my book.

Today, so many people – not just Sikhs or Indians but people from other countries, too – tell me they find it peaceful to visit a gurdwara and find that Guru Nanak's teachings bring harmony and balance into their lives. But the first Sikh Guru was actually quite counter-cultural in his time. Back then, it was only the wealthy classes who kept their hair long and wore turbans. Nanak and the later Sikh gurus (there were ten gurus in total and eventually the guruship was transferred onto our holy book) adopted these practices to equate themselves to people in the higher strata of society. He believed in equality and everyone, not only those born into the higher classes, should be treated like high equals. In the same spirit, Guru Gobind Singh Ji, the tenth Sikh guru, gave all Sikh men the name of Singh (meaning 'lion') because Rajpur royals used that name – later he also gave Sikh women the name Kaur (meaning 'princess'). Even the nomenclature of sardar comes from the title of Mughal army leaders.

My book breaks down the Sikh nature of doing good. Along with our distinctive visual identities and selfless acts of seva there are other traits and behaviors associated with Sikhs. In India, Sikhs have a reputation for being brave and standing up for the right cause even at great personal cost. They are also known to be happy-go-lucky folks who readily laugh at their own expense, despite carrying the legacy of a troubled history – Punjab bore the brunt of India-Pakistan's partition violence and Sikhs were the ones mainly affected by the Jallianwala Bagh shooting and the gut-wrenching violence in the wake of the death of prime minister, Indira Gandhi.

But through this all, we remain resilient and rebuild our lives through hard work. If there's ever a natural disaster or act of terrorism, Indians know that a gurdwara is a safe haven for them. Sikhs will be the first to offer help not just to fellow Sikhs but to everyone irrespective of their background. Of course, these are stereotypes but they do stem from some truth. I've seen it in my life and it was further validated in the research for this book. Each of the eight chapters in my book is dedicated to a particular Sikh trait: selfless service, joy, courage, resilience, humour, hard work, equality and positivity. Embodying them will help you do more good and also lead a better life.

Lastly, I truly believe that these lessons can benefit everyone no matter where they live in the world or what they believe in. You don't need to be religious to read this book; I rely heavily on evidence from the behavioral sciences to back my findings. So get ready to be surprised because truth be told, approaching life from a strong, ethical and joyful place is rather light on the heart. Seva is a solution that is as extraordinary as it is simple.

Introduction

Why Do Sikhs Do Good?

Think of any scene of disaster in India and you'll find a common thread: Sikh volunteers rallying to the site, feeding migrant workers, giving assistance to riot victims, and cleaning up after earthquakes. In the past year, full of so much difficult news, this 30-million-strong community stood out yet again for their extraordinary acts of kindness.

In 2021 alone, the media has reported some incredible stories on this very subject.

- The Hemkunt Foundation, started by Harteerath Singh and his family, set up oxygen langars in various cities like New Delhi, Mumbai and Kolkata to help Covid-19 patients when India was facing an oxygen shortage.

- Gurdwara Rakab Ganj Sahib in New Delhi launched the Guru Tegh Bahadur Covid Care Centre to make up for the shortage of hospital beds in the city during the pandemic.

- Bangla Sahib gurdwara in New Delhi launched India's biggest free-of-charge dialysis centre this year. The Guru Harkishan Institute of Medical Sciences and Research Kidney Dialysis Hospital, situated in the gurdwara complex, can offer dialysis facility to 101 patients simultaneously and cater to a total of 500 patients every day.

- In Dubai, a gurdwara trust worked with a healthcare organization to provide 5000 Covid-19 vaccines to people of all ages and backgrounds.

- Gurdwara Takht Shri Huzoor Sahib in Nanded, Maharashtra, decided to use all the gold donated by devotees over the past fifty years to construct hospitals and medical colleges. Currently, residents of Nanded travel to Hyderabad or Mumbai for medical treatment.

All through the 2020 pandemic, Sikhs reached new heights of doing seva:

- Since religious gatherings were prohibited, Sikhs distributed langar (the free meal served by gurdwaras to anyone who wishes to partake of it) and groceries via food delivery trucks and drive-through set-ups all over the world.
- Baba Karnail Singh Khaira, the 81-year-old head of the Dera Kar Seva Gurdwara Langar Sahib, fed over 2 million migrants on Maharashtra's highway in three months following the nationwide lockdown.
- In June 2020, the *New York Times* piece titled 'How to Feed Crowds in a Protest or a Pandemic? The Sikhs Know' highlighted seva done by American Sikhs in Queens, New York, during the pandemic and in Los Angeles during the Black Lives Matter protests.
- In Detroit, Shalinder Singh and his family distributed hundreds of pizza pies to front line workers like police officers, hospital staff and firefighters.

- The Dashmesh Culture Centre in Calgary built a vegetable garden in an attempt to bring people together in a safe, Covid-friendly outdoor space. The food grown is used in langar but can also be taken home by individuals for their own kitchens.

- The *Tribune*, Chandigarh, published a story about a Sikh vegetable vendor, Baljinder Singh, who has been doing seva at Khairuddin mosque in Amritsar for the past forty years. Every Friday he wraps up work in the morning and spends his afternoons looking after the footwear of the devotees praying inside the mosque.

What makes Sikhs do so much good, these acts of seva as they call it? Is there something in their values that makes them so generous, so giving? And how can the rest of us learn from them? This was the question I started this book with.

My understanding of Sikhi – the word we use to describe our religion – stems from what I saw in my home. My father was my first living, embodied experience of the philosophy. Growing up, I described him as 'Santa Claus with a black beard' because he managed to put a smile on my face every day. He is a quintessentially jovial, hard-working and sometimes scary sardarji, who taught me to always do the right thing. It is his personality and philosophy that have kept me close to my Sikh roots, no matter where I've drifted in life.

My mother spent her evenings kneading dough at our local gurdwara and encouraged me and my brother to distribute parshadas (flatbreads) during langar. Her motivation for seva came from the joy she experienced listening to kirtans – devotional songs – which quenched her spiritual thirst.

My nani (maternal grandmother) told my brother and me stories of Partition (between India and Pakistan), and we listened with wide-eyed fascination. We also learned that our papa had to stay home and not go to the office to be safe during the 1984 massacre in Delhi. But these tales weren't retold to incite hatred or seek revenge. On the contrary, our legacy of being protectors was emphasized. Kind has been cool among Sikhs way before it became a Brooklyn hipster motto.

Writing this book became an opportunity to look back and even investigate my upbringing. When you're from within the community, doing seva feels like second nature and you don't expect even a pat on the back for your contribution. So to begin with, I had to take a step back and break down all the elements of my upbringing that I had taken for granted. I delved into Sikh history and our rich storytelling tradition of narrating sakhis, parables about the lives of our ten gurus, looked at some of the cutting-edge research in science, psychology and behavioural studies, and conducted numerous interviews with Sikhs around the world.

I found that **you can distil Sikhi into seven simple, everyday behaviours or attitudes** that can be transformative for anyone. The first is the one we all associate with Sikhism – the idea of seva. Seva means selfless service, and in Sikhism it is not just an exhortation and a guide but a daily practice, just the same as cleaning the house or cooking. It is through their extraordinary acts of seva that Sikhs have gained the reputation of being the world's Good Samaritans, as you can see from the examples I listed earlier.

Going out into the world to help other people is entwined with various other values that Sikhi asks its followers to imbibe. Guru Nanak told Sikhs seva is as important as prayer, but he also told them to work hard and be mindful, to live lightly and smile – even in the face of hardship – to step out of their comfort zones and be brave.

Doing good is not an isolated attribute. Living a meaningful, joyful life is what fires the emotion of doing seva. That is why Sikhs lovingly fed langar to the very cops they are up against at farmer protest sites across North India. Ultimately what makes Sikhi – and the way Sikhs approach doing good – stand apart is the optimism, joy and resilience with which their actions are done. This positivity – what the Sikhs call chardi kala – is what makes it possible for Sikhs to give so much. I argue in this book that Sikhi shows us how doing good can be a celebration and not a duty. This is the Sikh secret to doing good. It's possible for all of us to make this shift in ourselves.

Now every religion teaches us to do good and be good, so why is it that such a high proportion of Sikhs do good? One central reason is the way Guru Nanak designed the religion. During his spiritual journey, Guru Nanak spent time with hermits living in mountain caves. Eventually, he rejected the idea of asceticism and, instead, encouraged the householder's role and told people to live honourably in and with the world. **Sikhism is thus created for our daily lives. It gives us guidance on how to live as parents, children, friends, employees, neighbours, colleagues and ultimately as fellow human beings.** Nanak taught people how to incorporate kindness, equality and hard work into daily life while simultaneously making place for relationships, jobs, weekends, celebrations and sorrows. He used a basic, natural simile to explain this to his followers. Live in the world but remain untouched by it, just like a lotus flower which grows in muddy waters but rises beautifully above them.

I must add the caveat here that I'm not claiming every Sikh is a paragon of virtue. Not all Sikhs are kind, hard-working, good-humoured and brave. Some are criminals and perpetrators of violence. I myself don't epitomize every single Sikh virtue. Sikhs, just like everyone else, are complex individuals, and when I refer to Sikhs doing or thinking a certain thing, I do not claim to speak for all Sikhs in the world. For the purpose of understanding the community's overall values, I make generalizations in this book.

The point is to study the Sikh way of life which offers wonderful lessons on how to be good in the real world despite having jobs, kids, social lives and health routines. I hope you find some value in unravelling the Sikh mindset – those of you who believe in religion and even those of you who don't.

It's hard not to be changed in the process of writing a book. All these years I was shaping narratives, but this narrative has shaped me. In the last decade, India's political climate had left me disenchanted with religion altogether. But while writing this book, I had the epiphany that Sikhism is not, in fact, my religion but my conscience. It has guided not just my life's decisions but also my simplest interactions from a very young age.

I gave birth to my baby boy, Azad, a month before I took on this book project and chose to give him the middle name of Singh. It turns out that when the time came to pass on my own legacy, I am as Sikh as they come. The seven behaviours I write about here are the values I will give him as part of his Sikh legacy. As we chant during ardaas (Sikh prayer):

Nanak naam chardi kala, tere bhane sarbat da bhala

(Nanak, with naam, that is, divinity, comes eternal positivity. With God's will, may there be peace and prosperity for everyone in the world)

Rule # 1

Help Someone Every Day

I must have been seven or eight years old the first time I did seva. It was at Dhan Pothohar, my local gurdwara in Mumbai, and I was ushered into the behind-the-scenes langar kitchen where the sevadars (volunteers) were cooking. My jaw dropped at the scale of the food being prepared. Huge vats of dal (lentils) and kheer (rice pudding) were simmering on industrial stoves, and trampoline-sized pans had 50 rotis toasting on them simultaneously.

I was given a basket of rotis and walked into the langar hall feeling rather shy and small. But within the first hour, I was gaily offering rotis to the congregation with loud calls of 'Parshada ji (Bread anyone)?' Rich, poor, young, old, all the devotees, including my proud parents, sat together on the floor and ate from plates made of dried leaves.

During my teen years, our family moved to Singapore and even there, every Sunday, we visited the Katong gurdwara where I did seva in the form of washing utensils. Sometimes this took hours and my shoulders ached from hunching forward. After one exhausting session, I loudly announced, 'I washed plates for five hours today.' My mother immediately corrected me saying seva was a privilege and not a chore, and I realized that boasting about the seva I'd done defeated the very purpose of doing it.

Only in 2010 did I get an outsider's perspective on this tradition. I was back at Dhan Pothohar gurdwara with my mother, and my then boyfriend (now husband) Aditya called me to make plans for the evening. 'I'm doing seva at the gurdwara with my mom, I'll call you when I get home,' I muttered.

My hands were clammy from peeling vegetables for dilkhush, a fresh, tangy salad that is served as part of langar. 'Oh wow, you're doing seva,' he said. 'I didn't know you were planning to do that today...or even that you do it.' I promised to call him later, and we hung up. Doing seva had been part of my life growing up, so I found it strange that he seemed so impressed with me.

Sikh families living around gurdwaras invariably find a way to make it part of their lives. My father visited ours every Monday morning to start his week right, while my mom was friendly with women in the community who routinely did seva. My brother excitedly woke up at 4 a.m. to go burst firecrackers during prabhatpheris (early morning processions) which happened on important occasions like gurpurabs (Sikh gurus' birthdays).

While daily prayers do happen in the gurdwara, seva is an equally big part of Sikhi. My father donated money to host langars on the death anniversaries of his parents. My mom took me and my brother along to help with langar seva routinely. I'd often get so immersed in my task that I'd forget about polite conversation. All of us would work in a steady, meditative rhythm, and when the tasks were completed, we returned to go on with our lives. It tickled me that the gurdwara managed to serve a 'snack langar' even for the people doing seva, usually tea and samosas. Even the sevadars have seva done for them. Such are the Sikhs.

Why do Sikhs do seva?

It's hard to be selfless. To be thoughtful, empathetic and generous. It's easy to write about these qualities, to preach them. Try to practise them on a daily basis and you'll realize it's harder than taking part in the Ironman triathlon, becoming a millionaire or looking like a pin-up model at 60. There's a reason why so many of us struggle to be good.

Five hundred years ago, Guru Nanak, the founder of Sikhi, understood this truth. And he created a radical religion that helped humans become better people in their everyday lives. He did it using a transformative idea called seva. Nanak identified our ego as the barrier that keeps us from an authentic existence and called it *hu main* (I am). Seeing the world from the perspective of 'I' keeps us from being happy.

His words resonate meaningfully in our increasingly individualistic and inward-looking lives. Have you caught yourself getting stuck in a replay loop of a fight you had with a loved one or worrying about what will happen in an annual review with your boss? Do you go to bed thinking about your finances or a family conflict that's eating you up? Redirecting your focus from your own problems to serving others can help.

'Taking the focus off ourselves seems to be health-giving in more ways than one,' says Alice G. Walter, a health and science journalist who writes for the *Atlantic* and *Forbes*. 'Much of our mental anguish, stress and depression is linked to rumination and worry-based self-referential thoughts. Transferring your focus from yourself to another might work to quiet worry and distress about one's own plight, much in the same way that meditation is known to quiet activity in the "me-centres" of the brain.'

Walton has a doctorate in biopsychology and behavioural neuroscience, and her advice makes sense once you try it. Transferring that me-energy outwards brings perspective to your own plight; your problems could seem small compared to other people's. Perhaps that's why **Guru Nanak made seva the song of the Sikhs.**

This epiphany is not unique to Sikhi. We see it repeated across various religions. In Buddhism, the practice of meditation is prescribed as a way of softening the walls of the ego and becoming one with the world around. But meditation requires great mental discipline. You have to still your mind, learn to sit quietly. It takes months, even years to build up a practice of sitting quietly for thirty minutes. On the other hand, Nanak told his disciples that it was through seva that they would find God because he wanted it to become the daily act that all Sikhs practise.

Seva is an action-oriented, instant balm to

our problems. It is rooted in the real world and encompasses all types of tasks, from preparing food for strangers, taking in a package for a neighbour or helping to fundraise for a local school. There are no good or bad jobs in seva. You get your hands dirty, and the action is its own cure.

Sakhis, an oral tradition

So Nanak said, and the Sikhs followed. Was is it really as simple as that? Most world religions have beautiful, human values at their core as well as wise solutions to man's unhappiness. So what makes Sikhi so effective in getting its followers to go from thinking good to actually doing good?

Some experts point to the fact that Sikhi only originated 500 years ago and deduce that Nanak's message has trickled down to his modern-day followers without too much filtration as a result. While this idea has its merits, I have another explanation for the ease with which large numbers of Sikh have adopted seva and made it their way of life.

Ask a Sikh friend about the stories they heard growing up, and they're likely to tell you that they repeatedly heard sakhis about their ten gurus. These simple stories are based on the gurus' lives and highlight the sacrifices they made for Sikhi.

They exhort Sikh children to be brave, treat everyone equally, believe in one divinity instead of multiple religions and to put their heart and soul into seva. The oral storytelling tradition in Sikhi is powerful because its morals are hidden within the story, making it engaging for children and helping them absorb these lessons unconsciously from a young age.

Scholars in children's literature attest that the stories kids hear and read in early childhood strongly influence their empathy and the cultural and gender roles they adopt. Stories help children develop a critical perspective on how to engage in social action. When something is learnt in this way, it becomes an unshakeable belief that can drive every action in life.

One famous sakhi that talks of seva is the Sacha Sauda sakhi or the True Bargain story. It goes something like this. Concerned about Nanak's disinterest in professional work, his father, Mehta Kalu, gave the boy twenty rupees to go buy goods that they could sell at a profit. On the way to the town centre, Nanak crossed a village where people were starving, thirsty and ill. 'No deal can be more truly profitable than to feed and clothe the needy. I cannot leave this true bargain,' thought Nanak and bought them water and food. When he went home, his father got upset with him, but Nanak calmly said he had found a true bargain (sacha sauda) by making the best use of the money. Even though his father struck him in anger, Nanak held his ground.

The science of being good

It's not just Sikhs who have unlocked the secrets of service. Science has plenty of evidence on the benefits of volunteering and giving. While the idea of gaining something from selfless service sounds counter-intuitive at first, think about the last time you gave a loved one a meaningful gift. You likely felt excited as you waited for them to open it and wanted to see their reaction. Giving lights up the reward centre in the brain, known also as the mesolimbic pathway.

This, in turn, releases endorphins – the hormones that fight pain and stress – and leads to what is called the 'helper's high'. That is exactly what eight-year-old me was feeling the first time I walked into that langar hall with a basket of bread. After my initial awkwardness passed, I began to really enjoy distributing rotis to the sangat (congregation). A warm glow enveloped me, and I felt a strong connection to the people I was serving, irrespective of whether they were Sikh or not.

The Greater Good Centre at the University of California, Berkeley, reports on groundbreaking research in the areas of compassion, happiness and altruism. They have published a white paper titled 'The Science of Generosity', which answers some pertinent questions about pro-social behaviour. I'm listing the key findings below:

- In the Stone Age, generosity helped us survive as a species. It is also seen in some animals, such as chimpanzees, bees, birds, rats and vampire bats.

- Volunteering has a tangible impact on physical health; it lowers blood pressure as well as mortality risk. On a molecular level, pro-social behaviour is linked to a reduction in the expression of certain genes, which could result in a smaller risk of developing inflammatory diseases. Inflammation due to stress is the leading cause of chronic diseases in the world today.

– Again, if we go back to the Stone Age where the threats to survival were enormous, such as wild animals and extreme weather, the increased expression of these genes was useful for survival. However, modern world stresses such as work- and relationship-related anxiety though less dangerous are unfortunately constant. This leads to constant inflammation, which causes chronic diseases in the long term.

• There is a growing body of evidence that links helping others with personal happiness. Giving triggers the release of other happy hormones such as oxytocin, which helps you feel affection for people, dopamine, which is associated with pleasure, and serotonin, which improves your mood.

– Some fascinating experiments have been conducted in this space. Male undergraduates who were asked to help others pick up stuff they had dropped on the campus reported an increase in their positive mood while those who were not asked to help (and didn't volunteer to do so) saw a small dip in their positive mood. In another experiment, participants who were instructed to perform acts of kindness for others over a six-week period reported an increase in positive emotions and a decrease in negative ones.

Generosity is contagious: it propagates within social networks, places of worship and workplaces. Experts in preventive medicine are now suggesting that community service is just as important for one's health as avoiding tobacco and obesity. Stephen Post, author of *Why Good Things Happen to Good People*, writes that giving to others alleviates symptoms and improves the health of people with chronic illness, such as HIV and multiple sclerosis.

Research scholar Khushbeen Kaur Sohi co-authored a paper about Sikh seva, published in the *Journal of Religion and Health*. The study analysed seva within a 165-member Sikh community and revealed that frequent participation in rituals like seva is correlated with higher social well-being and also gives Sikhs a sense of community.

Being part of a community helps us survive and thrive because a strong network helps in accessing resources and satisfies emotional needs. A simple example is how my father will buy car parts only from a Sikh-owned spare-parts shop, both because he wants to give them the business and because he trusts them more than he does other shop owners.

So if giving and volunteering have such immense benefits, why doesn't everyone do more of them? Perhaps because these findings are contrary to popular belief. We think we only want to act in our self-interest or in the interest of our loved ones. Participants in a study too predicted that they'd feel happier spending money on themselves. But it turned out that they actually felt happier spending it on someone else.

The common perception of human nature is that we have unlimited greed. But in reality we can be greedy in some situations and be extremely generous in others. Human nature is not black and white but encompasses many shades of grey. We can move from being selfish to being selfless and sometimes even be both at once!

Sikhs just choose to make selflessness a big part of their lives, inspired by their gurus' words and deeds. Later in this book I will ask you to think about values like muscles that we need to strengthen with regular workouts. For most of us Sikhs, this particular muscle is highly developed!

Selfless service can transform your life

Before I explain how to do seva, I want to put it in the contemporary context. For a community of 30 million people, Sikhs have had tremendous impact all over the world through their acts of seva. Gurdwaras across the world serve millions of people free meals every single day, but this work was especially crucial in the Covid-19 pandemic. As mentioned earlier, Baba Karnail Singh Khaira fed over two million migrant workers stuck on a Maharashtra highway during the first three months of the nationwide lockdown. The United Sikhs NGO won the hearts of the public by sanitizing Jama Masjid for the health and safety of its caretakers ahead of Eid 2020. In my research for this book, I discovered Sikhs who launched seva food trucks and who run community soup kitchens in all corners of the world. They got even more innovative during the lockdown and started langar via drive-through set-ups and home deliveries.

The Sikh Centre of New York served 145,000 free meals in the first ten weeks of the pandemic and also supported protests against the killing of George Floyd by serving langar to the marching crowds. The Khalsa Care Foundation of Los Angeles distributed 700 boxes of pasta to Black Lives Matter protesters in Pan Pacific Park, Los Angeles.

An infamous BBC interview with Michelin star chef Vikas Khanna in 2020 brought this tradition of langar to the notice of the world at large. Khanna grew up in Amritsar, home to the most important Sikh site in the world, Harmandir Sahib, or the Golden Temple. He was asked by a BBC television anchor: 'You've cooked for the Obamas, you've been on a TV show with Gordon Ramsay. But it wasn't always that way, was it? You're not from a rich family. So, I dare say, you understand how precarious it can be in India.' 'I understand, but my sense of hunger didn't come from India so much because I was born and raised in Amritsar,' replied Khanna. 'We have a huge community kitchen, where everyone gets fed. The entire city can feed there. My sense of hunger came from New York when I was struggling here from the very bottom.'

Khanna's powerful reply delivered with gentle ease and humility may have embarrassed the anchor, but made many Indians (Sikh and otherwise) extremely proud. While it appears that seva has become 'sexy' now (there's even a TV show based on it), remember that Sikhs have unassumingly made it a part of their lives for the last 500 years. Here are five ways for you to make service a bigger part of your life:

Start small: To make time for seva in-between work, kids, social lives and errands, you should start small. You don't need to enter a gurdwara to do seva but what you do need is a shift in mindset. Instead of saying, 'I want to volunteer,' say, 'I volunteer.' Set yourself a challenge to do one small act of kindness every day for a week, even if it's in your own home. Continue for a month if you enjoy the feeling of selfless service. Examples would include:

Monday: Donating books, clothes or toys

Tuesday: Cleaning out a cabinet for your mom or dad

Wednesday: Helping a friend or family member with childcare so they can get some me-time

Thursday: Running an errand or fixing a home appliance for an elderly person

Friday: Letting a random stranger take your taxi or helping them carry groceries

Saturday: Teaching your niece a new skill like using the computer or opening a bank account

Sunday: Baking a cake for a neighbour

Own it: Sikhs don't boast about the seva they've done but it is a big part of their identity, and they're very proud of what their community accomplishes as a whole. 'The more pride you have in a particular aspect of your identity, the more motivated you will be to maintain the habits associated with it,' writes James Clear in *Atomic Habits: An Easy & Proven Way to Build Good Habits & Break Bad Ones*. Sikhs are the perfect example because they use this pride that they feel about seva to reach even greater heights of community service and disaster relief operations. Be proud of volunteering and you'll want to continue.

Make it something you enjoy: An effective tactic is to tie seva to another ritual or event or experience that you enjoy. Sikhs typically visit the gurdwara on Sundays and on gurpurab days (the gurus' birthdays). They spend the days and weeks leading up to it preparing langar to serve everyone. Eating comfort food together for Sunday lunch or on celebratory occasions creates strong bonds for the community.

Find your own version of this. I know of an environmentally conscious couple who planned a beach clean-up to celebrate an anniversary and even hired a DJ to make it fun. A college mate of mine used to combine his vacations with volunteering activities like building houses for villagers in faraway countries. Instead of making excuses, make the effort.

Can't leave the house during a pandemic? Be My Eyes is an app that connects visually impaired people with a community of volunteers who help them complete daily tasks by lending them their own eyesight. It has nothing to do with Sikhi but everything to do with seva.

Donate: Then the question arises of whether writing a donation cheque has the same impact as physically performing service. The tradition of seva started in the sixteenth century, with the langar served in Nanak's first Sikh centre in Kartarpur (in present-day Pakistan). His disciples tilled fields for their livelihoods, then donated grains for the langar and also contributed time and effort to make a wholesome meal which was open to anyone and everyone who wished to sit on the floor and partake in it. Following in their footsteps, contemporary Sikhs too don't choose between these two things – they perform seva and also make regular monetary contributions to their gurdwaras.

But I can't deny that **there's certainly something powerful about working by hand. Talk to Kashmiri pashmina yarn spinners or Japanese makeup brush producers, and they liken the painstaking work they do to a type of tranquil meditation.** Even the contemporary self-care movement flaunts the therapeutic benefits of busy hands. As mental health issues gripped the world during the Covid-19 pandemic, my Instagram feed exploded with images of colouring books for grown-ups, endless loaves of freshly baked banana bread and plant-mamas gardening in kitchen windows and apartment balconies. So for true mental peace, find a way to do physical service.

I gave birth to a baby boy in the middle of the pandemic and was struggling with post-partum anxiety. One particularly bad week, I had spent hours crying about my breastfeeding struggles, fought badly with my husband and was reeling from intense emotions and mood swings. Not being able to meet my girlfriends didn't help.

So I ended up making a giant pot of biryani and distributed it to two colleagues who were living away from their families during the lockdown. Did connecting with them dissipate my anxiety altogether? No, but it did bring me some peace and improved my mood for the rest of that day. I can't exactly explain my own motivation for showing others kindness while I was hitting rock bottom myself. But what I do know is that eight-year-old me is smiling knowingly.

Rule # 2

Embrace Joy

Sikh Indian actress Nimrat Kaur's debut movie *Lunchbox*, in which she starred with Irrfan Khan, brought her into the media spotlight instantly. The very next year, she got cast in the American television series *Homeland*, and her life changed. Since then, this sardarni, who grew up in a simple Sikh home, has flown all over the world for shoots, hosted award shows, graced magazine covers and lived the quintessential celebrity life.

When I reached out to her for an interview in the early stages of this book, I wasn't sure where she'd fit in. Few know that Kaur lost her father when she was only eleven. He was an army officer posted in Kashmir at the peak of the terrorism years and laid down his life for our country. The actress spoke of her father with such grace and of her life as an actor with such candour that I had a bit of an instant girl crush, I must admit. Afterwards, I kept thinking about her story, the loss of a parent and then her rise to success in Bollywood.

'Nimrat, what do you do to find joy every day?' I asked. 'Well, I try to stay close to nature whenever I can,' she replied. 'During the lockdown, I've been waking up early to catch the sunrise, and at sunset, I go jogging by the sea. If I'm having a blah day, running by the ocean immediately turns my mood around. Cooking really helps me find joy too, especially if I'm cooking for loved ones or even just my neighbours.'

She continued, 'Cleaning is massively therapeutic for me, and I've been into reorganizing cabinets and wardrobes ever since I was a young girl. Praying and meditating every single day is also something I do no matter how tired or busy I may be. Sometimes, I'll put on my favourite music and dance away and even sing along. I live alone, so I have the liberty of blaring my speakers without bothering anyone.'

It was two in the morning when I heard her response, and I almost fell off the bed. She did all that on a daily basis to find joy in life? Maybe she should have written this book instead of me! But as I reflected on her words, so many similar Sikhs from my own life came to mind.

My mother delights in learning naughty folk songs to sing at weddings. My aunt eats with such relish I get hungry just looking at her. Practically all the men in my life (father, brother, husband) spend their weekends and vacations enjoying a drink, laughter and conversations. My film-maker friend Karishma Kohli uses music to fill her soul – she sings and dances to infuse her life with joy, healing and focus.

Sikhs are commonly perceived to be people who live life large but there's more to this idea than indulging in butter chicken and bhangra. **In the previous chapter I spoke about doing good for others. Here, I'm going to extol the virtues of having a good time yourself.** This may sound odd, but the Sikh faith doesn't see any contradiction between these two things. It is this very joy that fuels the Sikh nature to do good. When you're able to enjoy both the big happinesses and the small joys in life, your heart makes room to spread this good fortune to others. By embracing joy in their own lives, Sikhs are able to turn even service into a celebration.

Miri piri – a sweet balance

Most world religions usually proscribe or restrict the consumption of certain foods, include some form of fasting, require clergy to be celibate, and some even consider music frivolous or harmful to the spirit.

Sikhi, on the other hand, does not consider these things sinful nor does it glorify abjuring them. It encourages disciples to enjoy delectable feasts, upbeat music, vibrant dance and physical affection. Gurdwaras feed scores of people belonging to all faiths every day, music is an integral part of the holy book, the Guru Granth Sahib, and Sikh granthis (priests) live on gurdwara premises with their wives and children.

There's a marked absence of guilt with regard to lifestyle choices. I'm not trying to suggest Sikhi doesn't have any rules. But you don't need to offer flowers or cover your legs or confess your sins to be considered a good Sikh. Even our baptism, known as amrit chhakna, is an optional practice. This unusual philosophy goes back to the ten Sikh gurus.

Guru Nanak grew up in a time when the spiritual path was closely entwined with asceticism. Giving up familial ties to go live in the mountains and attain enlightenment was considered admirable. Nanak met with many yogis to try to understand their perspective but eventually criticized their choices. What are you doing alone up here in the mountains when there is so much misery among the people in the plains, he asked.

He had the opposite vision. He wanted

people to live in and with the world. So Nanak taught people how to incorporate kindness, equality and hard work into daily life and he conferred tremendous significance to the role of householder. He used a basic, natural simile to explain this to his followers. Live in the world but remain untouched by it, just like a lotus flower which grows in muddy waters but rises beautifully above them.

Later, the sixth Sikh guru, Hargobind, coined the phrase 'miri piri', giving importance to both aspects of life – the material (miri, from the Arabic amir, meaning wealthy) and the spiritual (piri, from the Persian pir, saint). When he became guru of the Sikh faith at the age of eleven, he asked for two kirpans (swords). One symbolized miri while the other symbolized piri. Even as a child, Guru Hargobind knew that this sweet balance was the secret to living a full life.

So it turns out that **Sikhs practically have a permission slip from their gurus to enjoy life, although with a strong spiritual component.**

They're good at incorporating both pleasure and peace into their lives, relishing tasty food, laughing easily and singing and dancing with gusto.

Eudaemonic vs hedonistic happiness

So Sikhi tells us to eat, drink and make merry, but this doesn't mean one can get drunk every night and participate in orgies. In fact, the religion frowns on any type of extreme, especially those fuelled by irrational pleasures. Search for the hashtag #yolo (you only live once) on social media, you'll discover videos of people hurling ham sandwiches across rooms and playing stupid pranks after getting drunk. These YOLO experiences are exactly what is not included in the scope of embracing joy as per Sikhi.

Psychologists will tell you that there are two types of happiness. The dopamine hit that accompanies things like the number of likes on an Instagram post, an online purchase or a compliment is short-lived: it ends when the stimulus peters out. This 'high', created by external stimuli, is known as hedonistic happiness and sometimes takes an ugly turn, such as a smartphone addiction or poor self-esteem. The opposite of this is eudaemonic happiness, which comes from experiences of meaning and purpose such as doing seva, learning a new skill or spending quality time with your family.

Does this mean we have to give up material pleasures like luxury vacations, exotic dishes and our favourite brands to be the right kind of happy? Not according to Sikhi. You simply have to balance the miri with some piri.

Some sardars and sardarnis drive big cars, wear flashy clothes and indulge in food and drink. But they also spend time monthly, weekly or even daily doing seva. **The Guru Granth Sahib speaks extensively of life being an opportunity pregnant with potential – 'This is the time, this is your turn'** – and cautions that to miss out will prove very costly. In addition to following Guru Nanak's tenets, Sikh men and women use this potential by living each day to its fullest in both big and small ways.

Again, science reaffirms this philosophy and says that for a human being to truly flourish they need both kinds of happiness in their lives. Psychologist Luke Wayne Henderson and colleagues published a paper on this subject in the *Journal of Positive Psychology*.

Their findings show that eudaemonic behaviours help us find meaning and purpose in life. But hedonistic behaviours can also be beneficial, leading to more positive emotions, reducing stress and depression and generally making people more satisfied in life. This thought has been echoed by philosophers through the ages; according to Maslow's Hierarchy of Needs, we can only achieve self-actualization after both our material and psychological needs are met.

Why is the idea of embracing joy revolutionary? While enjoying life may appear to be a basic concept, some people do struggle with it. Can you think of someone in your life who is able to laugh easily and claim joy? Now, can you think of someone who is the opposite? Someone who is afraid to experience the joys of life because of fear of the future and of other people's opinions?

'One of the biggest reasons people do not live fully is because of the deep need to protect their self-image of themselves,' says Mumbai-based life coach Milind Jadhav. 'It stems from a need to continuously look good in other people's eyes and avoid looking bad. The fear of being judged prevents people from saying what they want to say and doing what they really want to do. When I say people here I predominantly mean adults. Children below a certain age are quite the contrary and express themselves fully. They don't care about what people will think of them. And unlike adults they live life to the fullest. Most of us simply don't.'

Find your daily joy

How does one address this? For those who have the resources and privilege, it would be easy to book a trip, host a dinner party or invest in a cherished hobby. But not all of us can afford those things, and constantly seeing them while scrolling through our Instagram feeds can make even the best of us question our worth. Our bodies don't seem like the right size, we don't have an almost-famous 'squad' and aren't invited to restaurant pre-openings. Searching for happiness in the big things can sometimes have the contrary result, i.e., breed unhappiness.

The smarter happiness strategy would be to build it into your daily life. Being happy while on an exotic vacation is a no-brainer. Finding joy in your regular routine? Now that is truly revolutionary. American TV writer Andy Rooney (best known for his witty segment on the CBS news programme *60 Minutes*) has articulated this rather aptly: 'For most of life, nothing wonderful happens. If you don't enjoy getting up and working and finishing your work and sitting down to a meal with family or friends, then the chances are you're not going to be very happy. If someone bases his/her happiness on major events like a great job, huge amounts of money, a flawlessly happy marriage or a trip to Paris, that person isn't going to be happy much of the time. If, on the other hand, happiness depends on a good breakfast, flowers in the yard, a drink or a nap, then we are more likely to live with quite a bit of happiness.'

This is exactly why I was so floored by Nimrat's answer to my question about finding joy. She was mingling with famous folks on the red carpet and flying off to shoots in exotic locations but she was also revelling in simple actions like cooking, cleaning and dancing when nobody was watching. It's only once you are happy within that you'll look for ways to make other people happy too.

Sikhs know that to experience daily joy one has to live in the moment and be mindful. **So often we worry, work, plan for the future but when that future arrives, we start working for, worrying about or dreaming of some other future.** I'm guilty of this myself but was able to overcome this tendency in the past year. This is how I found my daily joy.

My husband and I chose to be childless for the first eight years of our marriage mainly because we were enjoying our life together too much to have it disrupted. While many of our friends were up to their elbows in diapers, we spent these years throwing parties at home and travelling the world. While zipping from one vacation to another and deriving happiness from the number of likes on an Instagram post, it is easy to cross that line from eudaemonic to hedonistic happiness.

After eight years, I was pregnant and, just then, the pandemic hit. Between battling the disease in our own home, taking precautions for a safe delivery and thorough newborn care, I started experiencing anxiety regularly. My appetite shrank, and I lost 14 kilos due to post-partum blues and not being able to meet my loved ones. In the absence of vacations with friends and fancy meals with family, I had to find joy in simpler places.

It's then that I turned to cooking and food to find my daily joy. However, this time, instead of going to restaurants, I used fresh ingredients to nurture myself through pregnancy and post-partum. My mother sent over a large tin of panjiri, a dry halwa full of good-for-you ingredients specifically fed to new moms in Sikh tradition. I began sharing my joy of good food by sending tiffin boxes to my friends. It was the joy of recreating and tasting my grandmother's flavours that drove me to drop off boxes of biryani to my colleagues in the pandemic.

Most importantly, I put my smartphone aside and spent hours cuddling my baby, despite having breastfeeding struggles. Instead of bemoaning the lack of vacations, I went through pictures of vacations I'd taken with Aditya over the years and expressed gratitude. Watching my five-month-old son touch grass at a friend's home for the first time felt magical. I returned quietly to the balance of miri piri, and since then daily joys are a part of my new life. In the following section, I suggest ways of how to find your daily joy through similar means.

Cook and eat with your loved ones – often

When was the last time you sat together with your family to eat a meal? Communal eating was once the centrepiece of family life, but today families have so much going on. In many cases, parents are both working and looking after the home, and children have signed up for various extracurricular activities or stay cooped up in their bedrooms. The smartphone addiction is rocketing off the charts, and, meanwhile, Netflix is luring us from the dining table to the TV screen with riveting content. There are studies that point to people increasingly eating on their couches and beds, while polls show that children and parents eat fewer meals together than before.

We can use this science to make small adjustments in our lives. Done every day, these tiny things will lead to big changes for us. British anthropologist R.I.M. Dunbar has confirmed through his research, for instance, that people who eat with friends and family feel happier and are more satisfied with life. They are more engaged with their local communities and have real friends they can depend on for support. Dinner especially makes people feel closer to those they dine with because it tends to involve more people, more laughter and reminiscing, as well as, on occasion, alcohol.

Communal eating is what has made Sikhi as popular as it is today. Sikhs will return home from early-morning religious processions (known as prabhatpheris), gurpurab langars and pilgrimages blissed out with their spiritual experiences but equally enthused by the creamy badaam milk, crisp samosas and tangy chhole bhature – delicious milkshakes and Punjabi snacks – that they consumed at these events. Eating together and relishing the food is as much a source of joy as contributing to making it. Sikh men and women regularly spend time, effort and resources to cook meals for the entire community as well as for strangers. Even the most discerning gourmand Sikhs wax eloquent about langar-wali dal, gobhi and kheer (homely lentil soup, cauliflower and rice pudding). Is it just the taste of the food or the joy of communal cooking and eating that permeates the experience?

How can you incorporate this value of cooking, eating and relishing the joys of food into your daily life?

- A no-phones rule for family dinners is quite effective. It forces everyone to engage with each other and talk about their day instead. Keep this slightly flexible; for instance, on the weekends, everyone can make other plans, and you and your spouse can have a child-free date night to reconnect.

- If your kids complain about the new rule, get them involved in cooking the meal, sourcing the ingredients or setting the table. You will all feel connected to the produce as well as to each other and will make memories for a lifetime. I have been showing my baby how our food gets made since he was six months old, and he loves watching the process now.

- Seasonal fruits and vegetables are a wonderful

gift of nature that we've sidelined in the lure of exotic ingredients imported at great cost to the wallet and planet. Get excited about seasonal produce yourself and spread this joy to your friends and family. Start pickling with your loved ones; shell peas in the winter to enjoy mattar-wale chaval (a green pea and rice dish) or make mango milkshakes to beat the heat in summer. Ask the elders in your family for tips and tricks – they'll be delighted to share their wisdom.

- Always remember, who you eat with is more important than where or what you eat. Try to make inclusive plans that are comfortable for everyone in your friends' group (with varying financial and family situations). Exotic dishes, opulent settings and rare bottles of wine are not as important as laughing with our loved ones and regaling them with stories. One easy way to do this is to start a weekly or monthly potluck club with friends, so you can all enjoy homemade delights and exchange heirloom recipes.

Make music part of your routine

Did you know that music has healing power? Several studies by neuroscientists and cognitive psychologists point to the curative and cathartic power of music and its ability to release dopamine in the human brain. It helps lower stress and anxiety levels, and promotes relaxation and better sleep. Music is also being clinically used to manage pain caused by chronic diseases like cancer, and acoustic shockwaves are being used to treat erectile dysfunction. Sound healing is cropping up at top wellness resorts all over the world from The Standard Spa Miami to Dwarika's resort in Dhulikhel, Nepal. I'll never forget perking my ears mid-massage on a press trip in the Maldives only to realize that kundalini yoga music – which incorporates Sikh kirtans – was being piped through the speakers. Buddhist singing bowls, echo and sound therapy chambers are all part of this wellness trend.

It seems the Sikh gurus were let in on this secret early on. While other religions also feature choirs and bhajans, the use of poetry, music, rhythm and metre is central to Sikh tradition. **Guru Nanak is said to have sung his way into people's hearts. Antique paintings of the guru depict him with his Muslim companion, Bhai Mardana, playing the rabab – an early version of the sitar.**

Since musical prayer is easy to commit to memory and creates a strong emotional connection with the hearer, the Sikh gurus chose to write their teachings as poetry and song (as opposed to prose). The Sikh holy book is essentially a compilation of these songs. Music has flowed from the religious kirtans and shabads (hymns and chants) to the vibrant bhangra genre, which has become popular not just at Indian weddings but also in nightclubs in New York and Berlin.

'There was a gurdwara right behind our home in Delhi and in our growing-up years we would wake up to the sound of kirtan every morning,' says the musician Harshdeep Kaur. 'It gradually became a part of our subconscious and helped us kickstart the day on a positive note. For me, religious Gurbani music is not just about Sikhism. It is a spiritual experience that helps strengthen my connection to the Almighty. Singing and listening to Gurbani gives me constant peace, courage and fortitude. When one is immersed in the magic of shabad kirtan, one automatically feels gratitude and humility. It brings an unmistakable sense of tranquillity and balance to one's life.'

Fortunately, you don't need to check into a fancy destination spa to feel the healing benefits of music. Instead try these six ways to incorporate sound into your daily life:

- Instead of waiting to play music when you hang out with friends, make it a part of your daily routine. Drink your morning coffee with your favourite movie score playing in the background or wind down at night to some soft jazz. My film-maker friend Karishma grew up practising maths problems to music and now starts her day with instrumental or electronic music while she gets ready. 'I listen to music without lyrics in the morning because it helps me think and visualize what I need to do for the day.'

- Sing along with your kids to gift them the joy of music. Write goofy songs about their personalities. I have an Azad playlist and turn it on specifically if he gets restless during diaper changes, and it always calms him down. If you don't have kids, sing in the shower for yourself. Even if it's out of tune, it'll lift your spirits.

- Make a playlist that you can turn to in boring moments like when you're waiting in line at the bank or commuting to work. My mentor Divia Thani (who isn't Sikh but believes in Guru Nanak's teachings deeply) plays French hip-hop to make her showers physically and mentally refreshing.

- Attend a live concert to feel a stronger connection to musicians.

- Learn to play an instrument if you're so

inclined – even if you never reach concert standards, it'll give you hours of pleasure.

- Try music therapy for better mental health. Humm.ly is an app which combines mindfulness practices with music. There are also trained music therapists who typically work with people suffering from autism, pain from chronic diseases, etc.

Say goodbye to guilt

If food and music are not your jam, that's okay. Find that daily thing you can look forward to. A new hobby like gardening or origami? Getting fit through bootcamps or dancing your stress away? Having a glass of wine to unwind at night? Finding your daily joy will help you experience eudaemonic happiness no matter what your bank balance, life phase or even the world circumstances are. That's an invaluable life skill.

A conversation about experiencing pleasure is incomplete without acknowledging that a lot of material pleasures like sex, alcohol and food invite disapproval from society. So much of our modern-day pleasures are tainted by guilt and shame. Even mild guilt can prevent you from embracing life's pleasures, and a study conducted on college students substantiates this. Students who were made to feel only a little guilty and then given a choice of free gifts in exchange for their participation chose school supplies from an array of products. Interestingly, those who didn't experience guilt chose movie DVDs and music downloads. Guilt can play a big role in hampering our daily joy.

But here's another way to look at this. Isn't wanting things the very essence of being human? It is the intrinsic motivation to carry on with our eat–work–sleep routine. Only when some parts of life are rewarding will we want to keep carrying on with our daily tasks. Who wants all work and no play? Nobody. It's about striking a balance. We can work out every day and look forward to cheat days; we can be diligent employees and enjoy relaxing vacations. We can look after our loved ones and also want to be celebrated on our own birthdays. It's the miri piri of contemporary life.

Have you wondered why watching anyone – even a stranger – dancing with abandon, eating with delight or laughing without restraint is an attractive sight that warms your heart? Luckily for Sikhs, their gurus gave them the permission to indulge in life's simple pleasures because they knew joy begets joy. Thus, they look at life like a blessing to be enjoyed, not something to hold back from. **They look at seva as a celebration, not a chore.**

Is that what you need? Then take a Post-it and write down this permission slip for yourself: **Experiencing joy is a small but powerful privilege of my time on earth.** Now stick it somewhere you will see it every day.

'The key to experiencing life's simple pleasures is to live like a little child,' says life coach Jadhav. 'It's not always easy with our busy, hectic schedules of adult life, but we must make an effort to slow down and just be. The way children experience little moments of bliss is what the real meaning of life is.'

Think about how children express themselves so freely and easily delight in ordinary things because they haven't yet learnt guilt. Something as simple as blowing bubbles or smelling flowers can seem magical to a kid. It's only once we grow up that judgements start affecting us, and we confuse expensive tastes for true happiness. Perhaps, then, we all need to unlearn our conditioning and channel our inner child. Take delight in the small stuff like eating a mango or hugging our parents. After all, life is a feast. Let's dig in.

Rule # 3

Be Brave

I began to have nightmares when I was five years old. I'd wake up frightened in the middle of the night and imagine a hooded figure at the foot of my bed. My nani helped raise me and my brother. Every time she put me to bed, I'd cling to her and say that I was scared of ghosts and monsters and aliens. She would instruct me to hold my kada – a Sikh iron bangle that reminds us of the inner strength of our God – and say, 'You are strong yourself because Waheguruji is inside you. Hold your kada and go to sleep without fear. Nothing can harm you when God himself is inside you.'

This small but significant ritual shaped who I am today. I was a timid and reticent child, so this message of carrying the strength of divinity inside me went a long way in making me brave – both for myself and for others.

Being courageous has helped me live with meaning and integrity. In my first month of college, I learned that a timid friend was being pressured to join a religious organization. Even though I was not the one being coerced, I confronted the person and asked them to stop pushing their religious views on my mate.

As a young adult, I worked for a digital marketing agency, located in a poorly lit, isolated lane in Mumbai. The company was generally tight-fisted, but I thought safe transport for employees working past 11 p.m. was a necessity, so I brought the requirement up with my supervisor – and I got it. In the first week of my marriage, I established that my husband's grandmother couldn't dictate when and for how long I visited my parents' home – a battle that some newly married women in India may not have the courage to fight at all.

Whether it is standing up to bullies in the schoolyards or protesting against authoritarian governments, whether it is the progressive act of refusing dowry or asking our own families to widen their perceptions of women's rights and roles, living fully demands courage.

On the other hand, the absence of courage exacts a price that is painful to pay. Consider women stuck in patriarchal families, people working under callous bosses and those unable to claim their own identities for fear of judgement (or even physical harm). Being unable to act on behalf of ourselves and the values we stand for takes a toll on our self-worth.

Those words my grandmother spoke to me before I went to bed were derived from her Sikh identity. They made me believe that true strength is an expression of the divine within me, and that it is my duty to listen to it and act upon it. They say what you are told as a child is what you tell yourself in adulthood, and that is definitely the case for me. I know deep in my soul that I am strong, and so even in moments of real fear, embarrassment or hesitation, I can push myself to act as needed.

From saint to soldier

It's not just me. Those who know Sikhs even a little know that we're considered a brave community. When the British arrived in India, they classified Sikhs as a martial race particularly because they admired the skills and demeanour of Maharaja Ranjit Singh's soldiers. They enlisted them in their earliest regiments, which quickly gained a reputation for being fierce and chivalrous.

Eighty thousand Sikh soldiers sacrificed their lives in the two world wars and over a hundred thousand – including my paternal grandfather – were wounded in battle. In fact, until proportionate quotas based on each state's population were imposed, Sikhs formed the largest chunk of the Indian army. Sikh regiments have also won the greatest number of gallantry awards for their bravery.

Movies have been made and books written about Sikhs displaying extraordinary strength against staggering odds. But the popular notion of sardarjis being strong is missing some nuance. While Sikhs have raw strength, they're also guided by a strong spiritual compass that commands them to use their strength for a fair cause.

Think about how Indian Sikh farmers protested against the new farm laws in 2020. They didn't arrive with swords but instead with tractors, six months' worth of rations and the will to stick it out for the long haul until the conversations went their way.

'Guru Nanak had a lot of moral courage,' says the decorated General Iqbal Singh Singha, who has led many Indian regiments and was also chosen to head the United Nations Disengagement Observer Force in Ethiopia and Syria. 'Our first guru would defy priests and royals to tell them how they were wrong. Our tenth guru, Gobind Singhji, on the other hand, was able to accomplish the work of entire battalions with a handful of soldiers, such was his prowess. But it was the sixth Sikh guru, Hargobindji, who gave us the balance of miri piri. Balancing brute force with a spiritual conscience has been a strong tradition in Sikhi. In the Guru Granth Sahib, this is termed being a sant-sipahi or saint-soldier. I think of it as the miri piri of the warrior.'

The birth of Khalsa

On Baisakhi of 1699, the tenth Sikh guru, Gobind Singhji, asked his Sikh followers to gather in Anandpur, where he was based. Once crowds gathered, he asked for a volunteer who would sacrifice his head for the brotherhood. A man called Daya Ram stepped up, and Guru Gobind Singh took him inside a tent. Within minutes he emerged with a bloody sword. He repeated this four more times until five volunteers had disappeared inside the tent for their 'sacrifice'.

In the end, Guru Gobind Singh emerged from the tent with the five volunteers safe and revealed that he had beheaded five goats in the tent. By asking his followers to sacrifice their lives without question, he ensured that only the bravest men were selected to be the first members of the Khalsa order. These five Sikhs were given the name Panj Pyaare, or 'the five beloved ones'. The Guru also gave all of his followers the title of Singh (lion) and founded the five K's of Sikhi:

Kes – unshorn hair to raise their status to army leaders and the wealthy class of the time

Kanga – a comb to symbolize grooming and the householder mentality

Kachha – long underpants to show sexual restraint when it came to women

Kirpan – a symbolic sword for their warrior identity

Kada or kara – an iron bangle, the shape of which symbolizes one interconnected universe and divinity

Courage = Seva

For countless Sikhs like myself, **standing up for the oppressed is simply another form of seva.** Thanks to our gurus' many sacrifices, courage, ethics and even spirituality are inextricably linked in Sikh tradition. This is what differentiates Sikhs' bravery from general ideas of force or violence.

In fact, the popular Sikh war cry, 'Jo bole so nihal, Sat Sri Akal', translates to 'Victory belongs to those who take the Divine One's name with a true heart'. Even in war, Sikhs channel spirituality in alignment with the all-encompassing divine presence. From Borneo to Pakistan to the world war trenches to individual acts of courage by contemporary Sikhs, the examples are endless.

During the Covid-19 pandemic, the Sikh community got incredibly creative about serving langar to those in need, both in India and abroad. They fought the fear not only of their catching the coronavirus, but also of further spreading it to members of their immediate family.

Risking your own death and your loved ones' suffering to be of service to a greater cause is common in the Sikh tradition. I think about Daya Ram, the first man who volunteered his head for the Khalsa order, or of Guru Gobind Singhji himself, who sacrificed the lives of his four sons in battles against the Mughal rulers, or the large number of Sikh army officers who have fought and died for India.

In 2020, India saw large-scale protests against the Citizenship Amendment Act, which granted Indian citizenship to persecuted minorities from South Asia such as Hindus, Sikhs, Christians, Paris, Buddhists and Jains, but didn't grant the same eligibility to Muslims. In the reprisals that followed, various Muslim-populated areas of the capital city became the sites of riots, arson and communal violence. Numerous Sikhs risked their own safety to save hundreds of Muslim lives. In particular, Mohinder Singh and his son Inderjit Singh used motorcycles to transport 60 to 80 of their Muslim neighbours to a safe location. Farmers from Punjab's Kisan Union also travelled to Shaheen Bagh, the pivot of the women-led protests, to stand with their Muslim sisters in the face of police brutality.

It's worth noting that Sikhs are coming out in large numbers to the aid of their Muslim brethren in India today, even though they have a long history of conflict against the Mughals. Who do you think they were inspired by? The ninth Sikh guru, Tegh Bahadurji, sacrificed his life to stand up for the rights of Kashmiri Pandits – Hindus from the Kashmir Valley who were being forced to convert to Islam. He approached the Mughal emperor Aurangzeb to speak out against these conversions and paid for it by being executed by beheading.

Guru Tegh Bahadur did not even believe in the Pandits' religion or rituals. Yet he was willing to sacrifice his own life, and even put the Sikh community in jeopardy by leaving behind eleven-year-old Gobind as heir, simply because it was the right thing to do, to speak up against injustice.

Our gurus' sacrifices cannot be overemphasized in Sikh culture. In light of their conduct, no seva or sacrifice seems too great for Sikhs. Sikh gurus set the example by sacrificing their own lives and the lives of their offspring, and so sardars and sardarnis are willing to risk their safety to go to the help of others. It is second nature to us, just like doing seva. Most importantly, Sikhs do the right thing for its own sake and not for any individual or political gain. Helping someone is not a partisan but a spiritual act. Nanak said selfless service is the way to be a good Sikh, and so courage becomes another form of seva for us.

Courage coaching

It's not just those fighting on the front lines of pandemics, wars and communal violence who need courage. Ordinary folks need it too. To profess our love to a potential life partner or to tell a stranger that we admire them, we need courage. To stand up for daily injustices and deal with judgemental relatives, nasty bosses, clueless friends, we need courage. To answer our true calling in life, whether it is writing a book or growing mushrooms on a farm or inventing a new way for women to pee in public restrooms, we need courage.

It's unrealistic to think that you can have an authentic existence without courage. **Because any transformation that can potentially uplift our lives comes with inherent risks, and to overcome those risks, we need courage, both physical and mental.** So how can you build this muscle? I've broken it down into four important steps.

1. Make room for your fear

The brain's natural response to fear and anxiety is to ignore them and do what feels safest. This is a biological, human reaction. Our brain wants a glass of sweet lassi before an afternoon nap, but what it needs is a Patiala peg (an extra large shot) of neat whisky (sorry, couldn't resist). So how does one get there? The first step is to acknowledge your fears because fighting them only increases anxiety.

A month before I gave birth to my son, I started writing a journal to document his birth and my post-partum journey. And soon enough, my writing tuned in to the anxiety I'd been feeling for the past eight months. The reality of caring for a newborn child had filled me with dread. While I'd been avoiding it successfully for the duration of my pregnancy, I no longer could. So I made a list, and this is what it looked like:

- I would not be a good mother
- I would not enjoy parenting
- I would not be able to breastfeed my child
- I would not be able to restart my writing career after becoming a mother
- My loved ones would not be able to meet my baby in the pandemic
- I would not be able to continue travelling frequently

- I would not be able to stay at my parents' house because of the pandemic
- I would have differences with the family elders about parenting
- I would get ridiculously fat, and my beautiful breasts would turn ugly
- I would age physically and mentally
- My grandmother's health would deteriorate, and I wouldn't be able to care for her

Not all these fears were rational or justified, but that is not the point. Writing them down let me articulate what exactly I was feeling. After losing control over my body in pregnancy, it helped me gain some control over my mind at least. I couldn't tackle every single issue, but a physical list of twelve fears in tangible form was far better than having them float in my head seemingly innumerable and insurmountable.

If you're feeling fearful of a particular situation or life decision, try making a list of your fears. Bestselling author Elizabeth Gilbert's *Big Magic* is about creative living and pursuing your passion. The first part of the book is dedicated to courage, where she wrote a letter to her fear about the creative trip she was embarking on. She gave her fear a funny character and also gave it place in her heart. And only then was she able to move on from it. Write out the dire consequences of your fears coming true. And remember, it is actually a brave act to admit your fears. It may read counterintuitive, but true courage starts by admitting that we're scared and then being brave in the face of it.

2. Find your why

I truly believe one of the most effective ways to build a habit is to align with your reasons for adopting it instead of focusing on the implementation. When you know your cause is justified, then you are willing to go to greater lengths to defend it. One reason why Sikhs don't hesitate to be brave is that they believe that standing up for a just cause is the honourable thing to do. This matters to them.

They would rather die fighting than be known as people who didn't do the right thing in a difficult circumstance.

So when you are mustering up the courage to fight your fears, one simple but effective way to motivate yourself is to focus on your cause, even if that cause is yourself. Once you believe what you want is worth fighting for, you will conquer your fears with greater ease. The strange thing is that I often find it easier to speak up on behalf of someone else, but when it comes to my own cause, I hesitate. It's only once we make the mental shift to believing that our needs and wants are worthy that we will start doing the same for ourselves.

One tangible way I find my why is by prepping for an upcoming difficult conversation and talking myself through it. Defending my case aloud helps me feel better prepared in an otherwise scary situation. It makes my communication more fruitful and clear, even if I'm feeling fearful or anxious in the moment.

I'll give you an example. I've been large-sized in various phases in my life and been fat-shamed by family, friends and even by people I barely know. These comments made me feel embarrassed and inadequate but also angry at myself for letting the bullying continue. I would cry for hours afterwards, and after one such incident, I realized I had to be prepared with a good response the next time someone commented on my weight, shape or size. So next time a family member told me I'd gained weight, I was quick to point out that fat-shaming is cruel and that every individual should be trusted with the responsibility of their own health. While it was unbelievably frightening in the moment (palms sweating, heart thumping, body shaking in fear), I was able to do it because I believed that I deserved better.

3. *Exercise your courage muscle*

Popular culture presents the bravest folk as fearless, but this is inaccurate and irrational. If someone is truly fearless, they may jump off a moving vehicle, put their hand in an open fire or walk alone in an unsafe neighbourhood. Fear plays a very important role in our lives because it prevents us from destroying ourselves in extremely stupid ways.

The idea that we are born strong is also a myth. Me and many other Sikh folks can attest to being shy and meek as children and learning to shed those fears through our upbringing. My parents simply pushed me to face my fears until I was no longer afraid. They made me talk to strangers, participate in school competitions and sleep alone in my own bed until these things no longer scared me.

'Courage is a habit, a virtue: you get it by courageous acts,' writes Brene Brown, the bestselling writer, academic and TED speaker, in her book *The Gifts of Imperfection*. 'It's like you learn to swim by swimming. You learn courage by couraging.' What would you do to get six-pack abs? A lot of planks? What would you do to learn a musical instrument? Hours of practice? Courage is no different, honestly.

Being a new mother was the perfect opportunity to live from a place of fear. My son had to have a hernia surgery and go under general anaesthesia at six weeks, and the experience left me feeling paranoid about his health. But living that way was going to be exhausting, and I knew that in the back of my head. So I made an effort to overcome that fear and practised being less afraid.

In the months immediately after, I would ride out the impulse to panic over harmless things like a morning cold or spit up and to call his paediatrician repeatedly. After three months passed, we slowly started seeing visitors and taking him to uncrowded parks, even in the pandemic. Today he licks everything in sight, and I laugh and say, 'Oh, at least he's building immunity.' Eventually, I did feel braver about being in charge of a tiny, defenceless human being.

Here's a courage exercise to try in life. **Pick a small to medium fear. Not a huge one that involves a major life decision, but something**

a little more inconsequential. For instance, the next time you are going out, put on that funky shirt or bold shade of lipstick that you've been wanting to try. Reach out to a random stranger through email or social media to tell them why you admire them. Visit your favourite restaurant and eat a meal alone in your own company.

Conquering a small fear will create some positive emotions of accomplishing a long-standing goal. The brain will eventually associate rewards with courageous behaviour and be less reluctant to indulge such acts. Once you've eaten a meal alone, the next step could be going on a solo weekend getaway. Once you've spoken to a stranger, you won't feel so reluctant to make friends at a party. Eventually you will start getting braver at facing and living life.

4. Find your courage community

The act of being brave doesn't always have to be solitary. There will be many moments in life, of course, when one needs to be the first one or the only one to dissent from the crowd, but not every single time. Sikhs share similar values, and so they're able to derive strength from their courage community in numerous situations, whether it is signing up for the Indian army or protesting against laws that they find exploitative. To know that there is a whole community that has got your back helps tremendously in standing up for the right cause.

You don't need to convert to the faith to apply this simple principle to your daily life. Find your own courage community. Are you scared of writing because you don't think you're good enough? Join (or start) a critique group with other amateur writers who want to get better at the craft.

Is there a social cause or public incident that you feel strongly about? Send messages to like-minded friends and associates about organizing a peaceful protest. Sometimes you don't even need an entire community. Just a role model of someone who is quietly courageous can help inspire you to do what you need to do. Psychologists believe that having a mentor makes people more successful in their careers. There's no reason not to apply this to your personal growth. In fact, Sikhs have been using their gurus as role models for courage for centuries.

There have been moments in history when simply being visibly Sikh with a turban and beard took tremendous courage. In 1984, after Indian Prime Minister Indira Gandhi was killed by her Sikh bodyguards, violence erupted in Delhi, where Sikhs were targeted, tortured, burnt and killed. Male Sikhs went into hiding and stayed home from work because mobs were coming into Sikh homes, dragging them out and killing them.

In the months following the 9/11 terrorist attacks in New York City, 300 hate crimes were reported against Sikhs in the United States because they were mistakenly assumed to be Arabs or Afghans. Racist slurs like towelheads were used against them, and Sikh men were killed by Americans who mistook them for being Muslim. On both these occasions, Sikhs bore the brunt of unjust retribution just to be who they are and go about their daily lives.

But they continued to wear their turbans and grow their beards in the face of all that with their quiet and determined courage. They derived strength from the community created by the Sikh gurus and also from the values they hold dear. Instead of boasting or talking about this courage, they set an example by not giving up on their faith – internally or externally – even in the face of grave danger. So, whether you're a new mother or a software engineer or a college-going student, adopt this saint-soldier mentality. It will help you live your truest existence.

Rule # 4

Say Thank You Daily

Hasmeet Singh Chandok grew up in Ludhiana, Punjab, and moved to Nova Scotia, Canada, for his higher education in 2013. The region has little racial diversity or awareness about Sikh culture, and standing out with his beard and turban wasn't always a pleasant experience. In a post-9/11 world, Chandok was often mistakenly assumed to be Muslim and even had a slur hurled at him in a parking lot. To add to that, he was trying to create a new life for himself and prove himself worthy in a foreign land.

But instead of becoming fearful or bitter, Chandok did quite the opposite. He started producing melodious bhangra videos set against iconic Nova Scotia locations like the

Peggy's Cove seashore and Halifax's Citadel Hill viewing point. These videos racked up as many as 50 million views in four days and also raised significant sums for Canadian charities tackling ALS disease, breast cancer and mental health problems.

The dancers' vibrant turbans, their infectious smiles and the lively beats not only introduced Sikhs to Canadians but won hearts in far-flung places like Japan and Saudi Arabia. Chandok founded the Maritime Bhangra group and became famous as 'the dancing Sikh'.

'We chose dance to represent our culture and also as a means to do seva because it is positive, happy, and attracts attention to our identity and culture,' says Chandok. 'We don't mention a word about Sikhism in our bhangra performances or speeches, but people can still feel our spirit of seva. They look at our distinct appearance, ask questions and eventually research about it on their own.'

Chandok is a living example of resilience as it is taught and practised in Sikhi. We know that Sikhs do a lot of seva, live life joyfully and know how to stand up for themselves and others. But what makes their actions and attitude exceptional is that they do so despite a history marred by war, loss and racism.

From Mughal invasions to the scars of Partition to the massacre in the wake of Indira Gandhi's assassination to senseless violence after 9/11, the Sikh community has suffered severe adversity. But they have on each occasion strengthened their resilience and overcome their setbacks by rising above them and being of service to others.

Can being resilient be any more important than in the wake of 2020? Everyone suffers adversity in life. Some lose loved ones, others lose jobs, some end marriages, some suffer due to natural disasters and yet others face tremendous cultural or societal pressure to conform to 'the norm'. If I were to leave the adjoining page blank and encourage my readers to write on it about their suffering, I am certain it would be full of heart-breaking human stories. To lead full, successful and healthy lives, we have to build our resilience muscle. In this chapter, I talk about how gratitude is key to prevailing over failures and overcoming hardship.

Resilience 101

From the Latin verb *resilire* (literally 'bouncing back'), resilience is the capacity to stay the course or even show positive growth in the face of adversity and risk. As a community, Sikhs have had to embody this trait in the aftermath of devastating and traumatic events like the Jallianwala Bagh massacre and Partition.

Many (including my nani) had to abandon their home overnight and many also lost family members in Partition-related violence. Today, Sikhs for the most part are a prosperous, cheerful community but they mindfully recount those experiences to inspire their future generations to build resilience.

As I started work on this chapter, it made me curious to know what distinguishes people who give in to despair in times of loss from those who rise above their circumstances to move forward. I came upon the pioneering work of psychologists Richard Tedeschi and Lawrence Calhoun who, in the aftermath of the deaths of their children, came together to work on a field of study they termed post-traumatic growth.

They observed that even people who had suffered through tragedies such as losing children, surviving sexual assault, fleeing war-torn countries or suffering from painful, chronic diseases could show positive outcomes in addition to feeling grief and stress. Obviously, it is understandable that anyone who's been through a traumatic experience will feel anxious or even depressed, but Tedeschi and Calhoun say they can also exhibit the following:

- Increased gratitude
- A desire to connect with people
- More emotional resilience, i.e., it is a muscle we can build just like courage
- An openness to embrace new opportunities in the personal or professional realms

- Higher engagement in spiritual thoughts and activities

I was struck by the gratitude point and it took me back to my mother's spiritual practice of shukrana, or giving thanks, which is a big part of Sikhi. Through my childhood, my parents emphasized remembering Waheguru in both good times and bad. In fact, **whenever I'm in a gurdwara, waiting to bow my head to the Darbar Sahib (where the Sikh holy book the Guru Granth Sahib is placed), I chant thanks for everything in my life** out of an old habit. My prayers mainly comprise giving thanks and surrendering to the will of divinity.

Today, gratitude is at the forefront of the self-love movement, but for Sikhs it is an old, life-affirming tradition. It's only once you look at your life from the lens of abundance that you can find the strength and perspective to overcome adversity. Getting bogged down by your personal problems is probably the biggest deterrent to seva. As you learn to surmount adversity, you reach a better place and are able to make room in your heart to help others. Even science backs this up with studies proving that resilient people fare better academically, exhibit lower delinquent behaviour, have closer community ties and have lower mortality rates.

Reaching out instead of acting out

The fifth Sikh Guru, Arjan Dev, put together the first version of the Guru Granth Sahib. It was a compilation of verses from Sikh gurus, Sufi mystics and Hindu saints in the seventeenth century. The reigning Mughal emperor of the time, Jahangir, ordered Guru Arjan Dev to remove the Hindu and Islamic references from the Sikh text as he felt it was blasphemous. When the guru refused to do so, Jahangir sentenced him to sit on a scorching metal sheet and had burning hot sand thrown at him. After five days of extreme torture, the guru was taken to bathe in a river and was never seen again.

Sikhs celebrate his martyrdom by doing a form of seva. During the summer months of May and June, we distribute a cold, sweet lassi called chabeel to the public in his honour. Instead of seeking revenge or shouting about this injustice from the rooftops, Sikhs mark the occasion by quenching the thirst of weary workers and travellers. Resilience, especially through pro-social behaviour, is a trait that is embedded deep in the community from the time of its inception.

Perhaps the biggest physical and cultural threats to Sikhs in the twenty-first century were the hate crimes committed against them in the wake of the 9/11 terrorist attacks. Sikh men in turbans and beards were wrongly taken for being Afghan by racist Americans and killed, assaulted and insulted with slurs. Less than a week after the American terrorist attacks, Balbir Singh Sodhi, a Sikh-American gas station owner, was murdered.

Following the loss of his sibling to a misinformed and racist attack, Sodhi's brother

Rana Singh took to speaking at schools and places of worship about the value of love, peace, tolerance and awareness. His outreach work has been applauded by Arizona's Anti-Defamation League as well as the White House under President Barack Obama's administration.

A family friend of Sodhi's, Valarie Kaur, was a lawyer at the time of his death, but after the incident she launched the Revolutionary Love Project to work with race and inequity in the United States. She is now an activist and a TED speaker who calls on her audiences to fight hate with love. For Rana and Valarie, positive emotions like love, compassion and forgiveness fuel their ability to get over the tragedy of the murder. To take it one step further to do outreach work against discrimination, thus helping all minority groups in the United States, is simply a natural Sikh instinct.

As seen recently during the 2020 farmer protests, Sikhs display resilience in tough circumstances. Large-scale demonstrations took place across Punjab, Haryana and

New Delhi in reaction to the new farm laws introduced by the Indian government. Sikhs arrived at the protest sites with trolleys attached to their tractors, rations for food and medicines and even equipment to set up gyms and salons. Do you know what else they did? They set up langars that everyone could partake in and did seva for the families living in the slums nearby.

Perhaps the biggest gesture of resilience was that the very same policemen who were battling Sikhs during the day were lovingly fed langar by the protesters in the evening. Despite the violent clashes where tear gas and water cannons were used against them, Sikhs overcame their anguish at the new laws by being kind to the very people representing their oppressors.

By reaching out to others from a place of joy, compassion and gratitude instead of acting from a place of anger or hatred, countless Sikhs like Rana Singh, Valarie Kaur and thousands of farmer protesters are simply taking forward the Sikh practice of using seva and turning it into a form of resilience. Their ability to do good isn't deterred by personal tragedy.

How I built my resilience muscle

The reality is that in times of deep despair, it may seem downright impossible to merely stay afloat instead of sinking. Reaching out to or helping others can seem too ambitious a goal when we ourselves are broken. The actions of a Rana Singh or a Valarie Kaur may appear to require superhuman reserves of strength, but just like courage, resilience is also a muscle one can build. I'm going to use an example from my own life to demonstrate how I built resilience and explain why building resilience became a life goal for me even in good times.

In the early days of writing this book, I was really struggling to get the tone and voice right. My editor kindly gave me a two-month sabbatical to transition my writing style and also get accustomed to being a working mother with an infant. She advised me to use the time to read widely. In that time of precious research, I made hundreds of handwritten notes from my extensive reading and interviews I conducted with various Sikhs. These notes were crucial as I approached the writing of the book with renewed vigour.

I'd finished a third of this manuscript when the unthinkable happened. I came home one day to find that the notes had been ripped up and thrown in the trash can by my domestic staff. Now, I am aware that this incident can't compare to losing a loved one or suffering financial ruin or sexual assault.

But coming on the heels of giving birth during a pandemic, having a close family member infected with Covid-19, experiencing post-partum anxiety, seeing my infant through surgery and witnessing my grandmother suffer two paralytic strokes, for me, this was the straw that broke the camel's back.

I was inconsolable and could not read or write anything for a whole month. Every time I thought about turning on my laptop, a debilitating paralysis rendered me incapable of doing so. Nanak's emphasis on seva stems from its tremendous benefits for our mental health. After a few weeks had passed, I knew it was time for me to do some seva towards myself to move past the obstacle.

In a desperate move, I googled 'how to be resilient' and started reading up on effective strategies. A friend recommended Sheryl Sandberg's book *Option B*, where she talks about picking up the pieces of her life after the sudden and untimely death of her husband, and it really spoke to me. As I processed my loss, grieved and rallied, I started to connect on a spiritual level not just with Sikhs but with any human who had faced heart-breaking adversity and lived to tell the tale. Building resilience made me more compassionate and empathetic and connected me to the entire human race.

The three things that helped me get over the loss of my notes were reframing the tragedy in my head, seeking support and starting to consciously say thanks often.

Reframe

In the immediate aftermath of the notes incident, I spiralled into despair as we all often do in times of trauma. I didn't think I would ever have the same chance at writing a truly excellent book again. Why had I not transcribed my handwritten notes into a Word doc as backup?

Who was going to give me a second sabbatical to reread those books and redo the interviews and make those same notes? How would I remember all the connections and examples I'd highlighted when I couldn't even remember the day of the week in my post-partum brain fog? What would I do when future chapters came back from my editor with major revisions, needing me to rework the pages successfully?

Popular culture stigmatizes setbacks and punishes failure. However, if one were to ask any group of people for the greatest learning moments in their personal and professional lives, chances are they'd point to the toughest circumstances that had made them cry.

Failed businesses, divorces, family feuds, working with bad bosses are all times when we've struggled madly but also had steep learning curves. In fact, many Silicon Valley organizations like Google, Facebook and Uber now openly celebrate failures. They're trying to normalize talking about goof-ups, even big ones, in order to encourage risk-taking and succeeding wildly which typically happens in the wake of crappy failures.

Sandberg points to psychologist Martin Seligman's research on resilience in *Option B*. Seligman is the father of happiness psychology and, after decades of work, he found that there are three things that stand in the way of recovery. The first is personalization, which is blaming ourselves for the adversity we are facing. The second is pervasiveness, which makes us believe that the adversity will affect all aspects of our life. The third is permanence, which is the belief that the aftershocks of the tragedy will never leave our life.

With this new awareness, I was able to

regain some control over my thoughts. I stopped blaming myself for not having an electronic backup because it wasn't possible to foresee the disaster. I looked at other aspects of my life where things were not failing miserably, such as my relationships or my finances. I also knew deep inside that I was going to finish the manuscript because it was important to me. Reframing helps you to look forward rather than dwell on the misfortune. I accepted that I'd have to turn on the laptop sooner than later if I wanted to finish the book.

Seeking support

According to the Tedeschi and Lawrence study, human beings crave connection with people after a traumatic experience. Making a list of people whom you regularly turn to for support is a great way to build resilience for whatever life throws your way. Often, having multiple people to support you is more valuable than relying on just one person in your life.

But there is a caveat to this advice. Sometimes

when something truly terrible happens, friends, family and colleagues feel awkward bringing it up because they don't know the right words to console you or find it hard to see you anguished. Conversely, we ourselves can bottle up during trying times and suffer silently, even when we are meaningfully approached by loved ones. It can be easier to block negative feelings than process them by talking them through. However, there are many examples of Sikh men and women who are practised in the art of being comfortable with uncomfortable conversations.

My friend Karishma Kohli lost her mother to cancer in the first wave of the Covid-19 pandemic. Since her friends and family could barely meet her during lockdown, we spoke over the phone. I made sure to ask difficult questions. How are you feeling about the prognosis? Have you cried enough? Are you bottling up the fear and grief? What is scaring you the most right now?

On many occasions, I had nothing to offer her but my presence. Discussing a dying parent is probably one of the hardest things to do but

Karishma was so human and open about it that she inspired me even at the lowest point of her life. She told me how she cried for hours while her mom lay in a coma. When her tears ran out, she played rock music and sang and danced by the hospital bed. Karishma is still deeply grieving her mother, but I know that being able to talk about her grief is helping her be resilient and cope with her loss.

The afternoon I discovered my notes had been destroyed, I felt a burning desire to call my mentor and seek her support. She told me I would need to dig deep and draw strength from the spiritual lessons I was learning from Sikhi and the research that I had done for writing this very book. I'll be honest, that advice didn't reach me in the moment because of how devastated I was. But after a day or so of mourning, better sense prevailed. I then reached out to more girlfriends who were forthcoming in their support and validation of my emotional response. All these conversations helped me heal so I could move to a better place and get proactive about being resilient.

Saying thank you daily

As I went through Sandberg's book, I wept many times. For her loss, for her young kids, for myself, for my grandmother, for Karishma. But I also gained perspective. I knew deep inside that dwelling on the lost notes for too long made it feel like an irrecoverable tragedy, when in fact it wasn't so. Nobody had died, and I didn't need to behave like someone had.

In the absence of religious gatherings during the Covid-19 lockdown, I spent a few days writing a gratitude journal. It looked like this:

- Writers typically receive tens (or even hundreds) of rejections before they can find a publisher for their book. The mere opportunity to write this book was a gift from the universe.
- While I'd lost my notes, I still had my loved ones around me. My parents were alive and my infant son was thriving.

- My grandmother was paralysed, but we had the financial means to care for her.
- My friends were supporting me emotionally through the misfortune.
- My husband and I had managed to ride out the terribly tumultuous phase of our relationship after I gave birth and were slowly making our way back to each other.
- My body was recovering fairly well after producing and nurturing another human being.

Giving thanks daily had both short- and long-term effects on my life. The first few times I wrote about the things I'm grateful for before going to bed, I did feel less anxious immediately and was able to sleep better without my thoughts going into a loop. Some days, I really thought I'd have nothing to be thankful for, but once I started writing, plenty of items would crop up on my list (from a kind word to a tasty meal to a crisp winter day). After a week, it started to form a habit, and the biggest impact gratitude had on my life was that it started the healing process for me.

In the long term, feeling gratitude helped me inculcate a positive outlook. When I practised looking at the positive, I had less mental space for my suffering. By saying thank you daily, I smiled more, embraced joy and countered my inbuilt negativity bias (the human tendency to focus more on negative events than positive ones). Savouring positive moments at the end of the day helped bring more positivity to my mind and life. I became appreciative of my family, friends and colleagues and also took the time to say thank you to taxi drivers and salespeople.

'The secret to living with joy is to stay present and to focus on what you have (instead of what's missing from your life) and that's gratitude,' says life coach Milind Jadhav. 'Acknowledge people in your life for what they mean to you. **Acknowledge every small thing that someone does for you and do not take them for granted.** This will transform the quality of your relationships and in turn the quality of your life. You will enjoy the little moments of life and participate in your relationships much more joyfully. Eventually this will keep you from getting into a complaining and self-righteous mode.'

There are plenty of studies to back these claims. People who give thanks as a matter of course are healthier than those who don't and they also live longer. They are happier, experience less depression, sleep better, have better eating habits and higher self-esteem. Expressing gratitude can make couples feel more connected and satisfied, it makes employees more productive and also makes people more empathetic and less aggressive. It is also, as I personally experienced, effective in overcoming trauma.

To build courage for restarting my work on the book, I took up small freelance writing assignments. This helped me regain my confidence and get back into the habit of research and writing. Changing the mental outlook to make gratitude a part of my attitude helped me feel abundance instead of loss. Once I had shared my pain honestly with my close ones, it became easier to think of myself as more than what had just happened to me.

Does that mean I got over the incident completely? No. Far from it. I still feel a wrench in my heart when I think of all my hard work washed down the drain. But do you know what else I feel? Faith that I have the capacity to get over adversity. And the perspective to focus on the abundance in my life, acknowledge it and give thanks.

Eventually, when I got back to writing and sent the next chapter to my editor, she said it was my best one yet. By finally writing the new chapter, I did what other Sikhs had done before me for generations. I had not only emerged stronger from my personal setback, I had also found a way to gain from it by putting these hard-earned lessons into a book. If I can do it, you can do it too.

Rule # 5

Learn to Laugh at Yourself

My father, a quintessential round-bellied, jolly sardarji, has charmed everyone in his life (including my mother) with his killer sense of humour. Even today, I meet old friends who remember his humour from our schooldays. I'll never forget an incident while we were on vacation in Krabi, Thailand. It was the monsoon season, and we had booked tickets for a boat tour.

On the way back, we got caught in a storm. The boat was relatively small and soon it was being hit by large waves and tossed around in the seas. I have terrible motion sickness and was vomiting non-stop, much to the concern of the other passengers, most of whom were non-English-speaking Chinese.

It was scary and tense. In the midst of this, my father mimed to everyone: don't worry, if the puking gets worse, we'll just throw her into the sea. Everyone on the boat, most of whom had been clutching their life jackets in terror, began to laugh. Our morale for the rest of the journey became much more positive!

It's obviously a generalization to say every Sikh is funny, but I believe that there is a grain of truth to this stereotype, and this is what we will explore in this chapter. Sikhs aren't just humorous, they also laugh at jokes made at their own expense. In fact, I'd go so far as to say they know the most sardarji jokes of all and laugh the hardest at them.

Being able to laugh at themselves helps them be resilient, embrace joy and spread it to others. While Sikhs are admired for the seva they do across India and the world, they're equally loved for the smiles they bring to people's faces with their humour and large-hearted jokes. In a way, humour is also seva.

In 2016, lawyer Harvinder Chowdhury

filed a PIL with the Supreme Court to ban sardar jokes – known as Santa Banta jokes, they poke fun at Sikh characters often called Santa and Banta. Chowdhury said her children felt humiliated by such humour and didn't want to take on the Sikh middle names of Singh and Kaur. However, the backlash against her in the media was mainly from Sikhs themselves.

In an article titled 'I'm a Sikh and I Laugh Loudest at Santa Banta Jokes. Why Ask for a Ban?' journalist Preeti Singh writes:

As a Sikh I have never felt there is malicious intent behind these jokes. Sardar jokes are not exchanged behind closed doors. Friends or colleagues don't suddenly hush up when I walk in on one. On a group chat, the Sikh members are not left out of Sardar jokes. There is implicit faith that the jokes will not be misunderstood; indeed it is Sikhs themselves who have a larger repertoire of these jokes to regale their friends with. (I have too.)

I confess to being baffled by this PIL. The

jokes do not undermine my pride in being a Sikh. They do not ridicule my religion, my Gurus, the Guru Granth Sahib, the gurudwaras or the *sewa* and *langar* in those places of worship. They do not undermine the beauty of Sikh women, our parents or our ancestors, or the turbans and beards the men folk sport.

When Aditya and I got engaged and our families were getting to know each other, he called me one day to narrate a funny incident. It turned out that his uncles, who are Hindu Punjabis, were discussing how they'd need to watch their tongues about sardarji jokes because they didn't want to offend anybody in my family, especially my father. In response, Aditya forwarded about a dozen Santa–Banta jokes to them, saying they'd all come from his father-in-law to-be. All his uncles were tickled.

Where others rush to defend themselves, Sikhs chuckle at their own expense. It's been proven that laughter is good for our physical and mental health (your neighbourhood uncles and aunties who guffaw as part of laughter clubs every morning will attest).

Laughter protects against cardiovascular disease, releases hormones that act as natural antidepressants and helps humans form bonds. Humour in communication can defuse tension, elevate status and help you convert people to your point of view. It's no wonder then that Sikhs are large-hearted not just in seva and courage, but also when they're being made fun of. Let's look at how this came to be and also at what happens when you're able to laugh at yourself.

Why Sikhs laugh

As a child I loved hearing our gurus' sakhis and often asked my grandmother to narrate them to me at bedtime. I particularly loved how Guru Nanak denounced the then worldly norms not only with higher spiritual wisdom, but also a sprinkling of wit. In my imagination, as Guru Nanak was presenting a revolutionary way of thinking and living to people in the fifteenth and sixteenth centuries, he was doing so with a little bit of tongue-in-cheekness. Millennials today call it the mic drop.

I'll give you an example from Guru Nanak's extensive travels. He was visiting a pilgrimage site on the Ganga where he saw pilgrims pouring water towards the sun so it could reach their thirsty ancestors in heaven. Nanak turned his back to the sun and began to pour water in the opposite direction. When asked what he was doing, he cheekily responded that he was pouring water in the direction of his fields to water his crops which were closer than the sun (which the pilgrims were trying to reach through their ritual).

Sikhs tend to live lightly. They face adversity like everyone else, but they have the ability to be happy and carefree (to an extent) despite it. This mindset could be attributed to their farming roots. When you're dependent on nature's unpredictable moods for a living, you learn to take life's ups and downs in your stride.

Another theory suggests that the numerous wars fought on their land and the experience of post-traumatic growth led to the funny bone being strengthened as a defence mechanism. Sikhs may want to live happily because they don't know what tomorrow could bring. 'Sannu ki?' is a popular Punjabi expression, which translates loosely to 'Who cares'. Sikhs can spend hours discussing something or someone they don't approve of, and they shrug off all the negativity with this simple rhetorical question and a chuckle.

This attitude can also stem from scripture: the Guru Granth Sahib advises us not to assume that we will live forever and to make each moment count. What better way to do that than by laughing with loved ones. 'The Sikh religion has adapted from older religions like Buddhism, Islam and Hinduism, and, as a result, is a simplified and refined version of them,' says Gursi Singh, founder of clothing label Lovebirds. 'There's a deeper understanding of lightness which other religions lacked or lost along the way. It tells you to live in the moment, to laugh and be happy and that there is acuity in doing so.'

Laughter evolved as an evolutionary tool among humans to connect with each other and thus survive and thrive as a species. A close friend of mine, Rahul, lost his childhood buddy to suicide during Covid-19. When I reached out to find out how he was dealing with the loss, he told me about running on the treadmill with tears pouring down his face and forcing himself to smile until he actually smiled. Science backs his strategy because the mere act of smiling triggers chemical reactions (release of neuropeptides and neurotransmitters) in the brain that make your brain believe that you are happy. A study published in the *Journal of Experimental Psychology* reveals that even forcing a smile may work to improve your mood.

Sikhs instinctively use the healing power of humour to build resilience. They know there's nothing as effective as laughing with loved ones to relieve a heavy heart. So they laugh at themselves, make everyone around them chuckle through life and even joke about its burdens. Sikhs do seva with a smile and smile to do seva. For them, humour is strongly interconnected with doing good, and **the truth is that when you're looking for reasons to giggle, no matter how hard your journey, you'll find many reasons to smile.**

Laugh at yourself but know your self-worth

In India, there are Gujarati jokes and Muslim jokes and Malayali jokes, but none are as ubiquitous as sardarji jokes. People across India don't hesitate to say, 'Don't be a sardar' or 'Baarah baj gaye kya?' (Literally, has it struck midnight? Apparently, Sikhs go crazy at that hour.) And yet Sikhs, for the most part, take all these jibes at their intellect in their stride.

The ability to not take themselves too seriously is strongly tied to Sikhs' idea of self-worth. Sikhs do incredible amounts of seva not just for themselves but for all communities in India and for cultures all over the world. They risk their lives for others in the army or as part of rescue missions in disaster zones. They open the doors to their gurdwaras to people of all faiths especially in times of need, like floods and terrorist attacks.

They do all this despite a history of war with the Mughals, experiencing Partition-related violence and atrocities like the Jallianwala Bagh massacre, the 1984 riots and the 9/11 hate crimes. They are secure in their idea of themselves, so a few small jokes don't have the power to dent their egos. If you think about it, Sikhs have been given the honorific 'sardarji' with 'ji' at the end of 'sardar' because there is inherent respect in India for what we do and believe in.

'In comedy, there's this concept of punching up,' says Indian stand-up comedian Vikramjit Singh. 'It's when you make a joke on someone stronger than you because they can take it. That's why jokes on political leaders and celebrities are popular, because they're in a position of privilege, and people on the lower end of the spectrum borrow some power by laughing at them. By that logic, Sikhs take it in their stride because they're strong enough to warrant it. It's the weak that can't take a joke.'

Having a strong sense of self-worth seeps into many other aspects of my life besides humour. I value myself and so I stand up for myself in romantic relationships and I also demand respect from my friends and family, including the elders. After years of hesitation, I now ask for fair compensation for my writing because I have faith in a decade of experience. I don't hesitate to express dissent in conversations and meetings because I believe even my contrary opinion matters. I have no problem investing in myself or saying no to people. It helps me live with joy and summon the courage to do what I need to do for myself.

I also do these things with a dash of humour. For instance, in my younger days, friends used to make fun of the fact that I left parties before midnight to go to bed. Instead of getting offended, I took on this jibe about ghosting at parties with happiness. I claimed myself a 'ghoster' and joked about texting my husband from the car, being an old lady happy in her blanket and how hard it is to say rational goodbyes after everyone at the party has had a few drinks. Everyone has adjusted expectations, and we all laugh together, instead of them laughing at me or, worse, behind my back.

Use humour to communicate better

The big difference in how Sikhs use humour is that they use it to communicate well and build relationships. **Being funny builds trust and also makes people more open to one's point of view.** Joking is part of our lives – with strangers in elevators and Chinese tourists on boats, during happy as well as hard times, while drinking with friends or conversing in the workplace. Many Indians will attest to having a cheerful Sikh friend or co-worker who laughs easily and makes others laugh too. Professors Jennifer Aaker and Naomi Bagdonas have written an entire book on this subject titled *Humor, Seriously: Why Humor Is a Secret Weapon in Business and Life*.

'Humour is a particularly potent elixir for trust,' Bagdonas said in a communications podcast. 'When we laugh with someone, be it in person or even over screens through Zoom, what happens is our brains release the hormone oxytocin, and we're essentially cued to form an emotional bond with that person. And oxytocin, by the way, is the same hormone that's released during sex and childbirth. Both moments when, from an evolutionary perspective, we benefit from feelings of closeness and trust.'

It also turns out that there's no better weapon to lower people's defences than humour, according to researcher Madelijn Strick and her co-writers who published a paper titled 'Those Who Laugh Are Defenseless: How Humour Breaks Resistance to Influence' in the *Journal of Experimental Psychology.* Messaging delivered with humour is received with less scepticism than that delivered without humour, according to this research. I'll give you an example from within my family. My cousin's husband grew up with his mother believing men shouldn't enter the kitchen. At a dinner in my home, someone asked him to fetch a knife from the kitchen, and his mother was present too. Her facial expression couldn't hide her horror at the fact that the son-in-law of the family was being asked to help with domestic work. But we simply turned the incident into a joke, and being a true-blue Punjabi, he guffaws loudest at it even today. Everyone in the family is more receptive to the idea of men pitching in with domestic work when we are laughing rather than fighting about the topic.

While the common perception is that humour is unimportant or even inappropriate in business settings, research has something else to say. 'Many believe that humour simply has no place amidst serious work,' Aaker says.

'We're worried about harming our credibility and not being taken seriously. And yet in large-scale studies that we run and that others have run, the large majority of leaders really prefer employees with a sense of humour and believe that employees with a sense of humour do better work. Showing your sense of humour can make peers attribute even more perceptions of confidence and status to us and vote us into leadership roles.'

So whether it's a boardroom or a bar, being funny will help you gain trust and be more empathetic towards other people. It forges intangible but powerful connections, makes communication more fruitful and breaks down boundaries. Once we relate to other people's stories, then going one step further to be kind, help out and do seva feels natural and joyful, instead of just a religious obligation.

Humour as a social tool

'Humour could mean different things to different people and cultures,' says Vikramjit

Singh. 'For some, it's a coping mechanism in adversity. It can do everything from enlivening a friendship to spicing up a relationship, persuading consumers and even threatening rulers.'

Centuries ago, court jesters could say to kings what nobody dared to otherwise. In contemporary society, comedians play this role while delivering political commentary. Subversive humour has been used as a tool against oppressive regimes for centuries, and this is why rulers and governments are more threatened by comedians than by journalists.

When you hear a comedian make a joke about an idea that you previously considered 'sacred' and laugh at it, even this untouchable religious, moral or national thing becomes just an idea for just a little bit. You may not agree with it but making a joke plants the seed in your head that it's not as powerful as you thought it to be. And in the moment that you laughed there was a tacit and unconscious agreement with at least part of what the comedian was saying. This is why conservative rulers are especially threatened by laughter, because it has the potential to strip the 'holy' things of their power over you. The Indian right-wing's reactions to comedians, for instance, sound familiar in this context. But sometimes the tables also turn: in the Ukraine's 2019 elections, comedian Volodymyr Zelensky won the presidency by a landslide.

Cartoonist Dashmeet Singh lives in New Delhi but travelled to the capital's Singhu and Tikri borders as part of a documentary crew covering the nationwide farmers' protests in 2021. His testimony speaks to how humour can be a coping mechanism for individuals and also gives motivation and power to social movements that question government policies.

'If you spend a few hours with these farmers, they'll start off by airing their grievances and unloading their hearts,' he says. 'But eventually their Sikh traits reveal themselves. The farmers continued the protests through North India's harsh winter without a roof over their heads. They were able to do it because of their resilience to tough circumstances and they eventually even started making light-hearted jokes about their adverse conditions.'

So how do we add more humour to our lives? The experts in this chapter weigh in.

1. **Laugh more:** According to Aaker and Bagdonas, the simplest step is to be more generous with your laughter. 'It's our point of view that when you walk around on the precipice of a smile, you will be surprised by how many things you encounter that will push you over the edge,' Bagdonas says. This is something Sikhs are good at and is fairly easy for anyone to implement. A funny story, joke or even seeing someone else roar with laughter can often produce at least a chuckle if not a full-blown laugh from me.

2. **Notice your own idiosyncrasies:** Dashmeet Singh says his humour comes from examining his own life. 'As an artist, I simply observe things carefully and put it on a canvas,' he

says. 'My comics are a documentation of my daily life and my happy moments. Everyone has these experiences, but the moments are so tiny that people tend to miss them. Cartoons are exaggerated by nature, but my work always stems from some truth of my daily life.' If you really want to be a funnier person and make people laugh, go through the day making a list of these tiny things from your own life. Mine would look like this:

1. When I wake up, I'm more excited to make my cup of coffee than wish my husband good morning.

2. I brush after breakfast not before because I can't stand breakfast-breath of masala omelette, dosa chutney and the like.

3. Being hangry is a real thing with me, and I'm especially crabby right before mealtimes (hence those who present a contrary opinion right then may suffer my wrath).

4. I'll refuse to wear a watch even though

I always want to know what time it is. Instead, I bug my family and friends by constantly asking them.

5. My water bottle is as dear to me as my firstborn child.

6. I'm clumsy as hell, often break things and will bang my toes and elbows on pieces of furniture just walking through the house.

3. **Make your misery amusing:** Here's my two cents. Self-deprecatory humour comes from having high self-worth, as we discussed, but also plays a crucial role in keeping your ego in check – one of Nanak's central concerns. People who can laugh at themselves instead of getting uncomfortably embarrassed when they fumble in public are typically well adjusted. They know they are as big or as small as anyone else and yet they're endearing because they become more human in the eyes

of the audience. Humour can thus become a tool in taking risks, making mistakes and making friends.

For six months after giving birth, I suffered from post-partum anxiety which took a toll on my marriage, career, relationships and personality. Since self-deprecatory humour is second nature to me, I soon began to make jokes about the hormones raging, mood swings and sleepless nights. I spoke of these things on Instagram, comparing my baby's noisy breathing to a jungle soundtrack or switching characters from doting mother to angry lady in one swipe. Laughing alongside crying started the healing process for me. People started reaching out to laugh with me mostly but also asked questions or told me that they admire my humour and candidness. I am now part of an online community of mothers who are living the circus daily, just like me.

So learn to laugh at yourself like the Sikhs do. It'll keep you healthy, build your resistance to adversity and even make you popular for all the right reasons.

Rule # 6

Practise Equality at Home

If you've never eaten langar in a gurdwara, put it on your bucket list – India has scores of them, of course, but Sikh communities have built gurdwaras wherever they've settled in the world, from Parma, Italy to Katong, Singapore. You'll remember forever the hot splatter of kali dal falling on your plate and the sevadars insisting that you eat some aromatic kheer before you go. It is the taste of my childhood.

Every Sunday, after attending prayers upstairs in the gurdwara, we would enter the langar hall, everyone would sit together on the floor and wait to be served. Kirtan music would play in the background, and little Sikh boys and girls would enter with buckets of food, easy smiles and calls of 'Parshada ji' for rotis and 'Dilkhush ji' for salad. I'd go back home with my stomach and heart full.

Sikhs take pride in the fact that people from all castes, economic backgrounds and religious affiliations sit on the floor to eat together. As a child, I would boast to my schoolmates that millionaires and beggars eat side by side in my place of worship. I was always curious to see who would be sitting beside me during langar.

Sometimes it would be a homeless family that had been starving all day; other times I'd see the neighbourhood aunty there, loading up her tiffin to avoid cooking dinner. My mother once found herself seated back to back with our own house help, and as an adolescent, I sat next to an Australian backpacker to whom I went on to explain the concept of seva and then each dish we were served. It didn't matter who we were and where we came from – for the duration of that meal, we became a fraternity.

The langar setting demonstrates beautifully

how embedded the idea of equality is in Sikh scripture and culture. Sikhi doesn't differentiate much between people. It's never turned away people belonging to so-called lower castes or those who are hungry and homeless. Women don't need to mark their marital status or cover up. In fact, the onus of our visual identity lies more with men, because of the turbans and beards they sport.

There's no prohibition on entering the gurdwara if you're menstruating. To mitigate income inequality, the Guru Granth Sahib suggests giving dashwant, i.e., donating 10 per cent of our income to charity. Accordingly, Sikhs give generously to their gurdwaras, which use funds to feed people langar and set up medical camps.

This is remarkable because even on an individual level people have work to do when it comes to equal treatment. It's far easier to talk about practising equality in society at large than it is to actually commit to and live by it in your own home.

Once we scratch the surface, it turns out that being philanthropic or preaching equality on a general and societal level is in some ways easier than enacting it constantly and consistently at home. When we have to face our biases within our personal spaces and our relationships, looking them in the eye can be far more difficult. Treating people equally irrespective of their religion, economic background, gender, race and class is quite an unusual teaching for a world religion to propagate; I'd say Sikhi is Sikhi because of this idea. **The acceptance of all humans being equal and worthy is what makes Sikhs put out so much good into the world.**

Why is it important for us to be equal as individuals and as a society? There's a mountain of research that points to equitable societies having better physical and mental health. Look at statistics on lifestyle diseases, mental health issues and suicide rates, or just speak to people around you. We live in an ever-connected world, but people still feel lonely.

What comes as a bit of a surprise is that economic growth alone cannot resolve this problem. Studies show that material wealth does improve health and happiness among people, but only to a certain extent. While public goods and services like vaccinations and access to safe drinking water and food are directly related to the well-being of countries and societies, once our basic needs are met and we've reached a certain level of affluence, money cannot buy us more happiness. But equality can.

Nanak's egalitarian dream

Guru Nanak instinctively knew the benefits of equality centuries before science or social studies supported the idea. Nanak is said to have achieved enlightenment after disappearing into the river Beas for a few days. When he came out, the first words he uttered were, Ik Omkar, i.e., there is one divinity and it is connected to the entire universe, including all human beings. The Sikh community believes wholly in this idea.

Believing in equality and practising it helps you embrace the 'other' as yourself. It helps us become part of a fraternity of humanity and thus motivates us to engage in selfless service.

'Sikhs pray daily for "Sarbat da Bhala", i.e., the well-being of all, and the faith recognizes all of humanity as one,' says Ravi Singh, founder of Khalsa Aid, a humanitarian organization known for sending first response teams to sites of natural and man-made disasters such as floods, earthquakes, famines and wars. For him, **seva naturally arises when we treat people equally**, or when we, as Nanak said, embrace the other. 'It's only once we see everyone as one and treat everyone with respect and dignity regardless of race, religion or borders, that there can be selfless service with no expectation of reward.'

Guru Nanak was quite counter-cultural. His vision of a classless community threatened the prevalent caste system and all-powerful monarchies. The seeds of conflict between the

Sikhs and the Mughals were sown because of his egalitarian thought. Our later gurus ensured that Sikhi is quite diverse in its origins, and perhaps that's why it is open to treating people from all backgrounds equally. In the spirit of inclusivity, Sikhi incorporated verses from Hindu saints and Muslim mystics in the Guru Granth Sahib, which was originally written in numerous languages, such as Sanskrit, Urdu and Persian.

When the tenth Sikh guru, Gobind Singh, started the Khalsa order, he ensured that his men wore turbans and gave them the name of Singh, which means lion. At the time, only Mughal army leaders wore turbans and high-ranking Rajputs used the title Singh, but Guru Gobind Singh wanted to make this visual identity and nomenclature common among his men. Within the Khalsa order, men belonging to lower castes were often promoted to leadership roles, which was very unusual in the seventeenth century.

Women such as Mai Bhago, Jind Kaur, Sada Kaur and Bibi Sahib Kaur battled alongside men, first against the Mughal army and later against the British in undivided Punjab. 'The Darbar Sahib [Golden Temple] foundation was laid by a Muslim pir of Lahore,' writer Tavleen Singh reminded me when I asked her to weigh in on the subject. 'Nanak was heavily influenced by Sufi saints, and I'd go so far as to say that Sikhism is the only Sufi religion in the world. Yet all of our gurus were born Hindus. The faith's very origins are of mixed tradition.'

She continued, 'Back in the days when it was possible, I was crossing from Lahore to Amritsar by car and had a Pakistani friend with me. She said she'd never seen the Golden Temple, so I took her to visit. When we knelt in front of the Guru Granth Sahib, she said her Muslim prayers. But the surprising part was that nobody in the gurdwara turned a hair at the sight of a Muslim woman doing namaz in a Sikh gurdwara.'

Sakhi: Bhai Kanhaiya, the true Sikh

One sakhi that illustrates Guru Gobind Singh's commitment to equality is set in the seventeenth century when the fights between the Sikhs and Mughals had intensified. At dusk, when both armies had called ceasefire for the day, a Sikh by the name of Bhai Kanhaiya went around the battlefield, strewn as it was with corpses, and quenched the thirst of wounded soldiers with his mashak (water pouch). He made no differentiation between the Sikh and Mughal soldiers.

This angered the Sikh soldiers because the city had been surrounded and food and water supplies were scarce. They escalated the issue to Guru Gobind Singh, calling Bhai Kanhaiya a traitor. When asked about his actions, Bhai Kanhaiya simply said he was observing Nanak's guidelines of embracing the other (in this case, the enemy) as himself and doing seva for them. Guru Gobind Singh was so touched by this response that he praised Bhai Kanhaiya instead of punishing him and let him go about his business of doing seva.

How does one champion equality? It's a big question. When we talk of equality, we are talking of the relationships between men and women, rich and poor, upper and lower classes. Ultimately, lobbying for equal policies and more representation in government is key to making large-scale societal changes. But each one of us can bring about real change at a grassroots level. Only once we practise equality with our own partners, sons, daughters, daughters-in-law, relatives and people who work with and for us at every level can we preach it to others. If the only thing we can really control is our own behaviour inside the home, let us start there.

Address the biggest concern – domestic work

One of the biggest ways the gender divide manifests in the family is through the share of housework done by men versus women. It's impossible to preach equality without addressing this topic. Increasingly, men in India and around the world want workplace equality for the sexes and even advocate for equal pay, but in a contradictory pattern, they are unwilling to share duties at home. There is a strong cultural bias that men are required to bring home a salary and then do nothing to help out with domestic chores.

The amount of housework that men do in comparison to their wives, mothers, sisters and daughters is appallingly little. According to a 2020 report by the National Statistics Office, the average Indian woman dedicates 243 minutes (around four hours) a day to domestic activities. On the contrary, the average man dedicates 25 minutes to housework – that's one-tenth of what women do! In Britain, women did 60 per cent more unpaid domestic work that men (according to the Office of National Statistics in 2016). In the US, women do twice as much domestic work and childcare as their male counterparts (according to a 2012 paper in Social Forces academic journal). As a result, men have more time to spend on activities like working, studying and, yes, even self-care.

What is the price women pay for this? They don't find the time required to work in higher-salaried jobs or sometimes they don't find the time to work at all. Not bringing in an income prevents them from being equal decision-makers in their own family and perpetuates a vicious cycle. It has a tangible effect on their physical health too.

Seventy-one per cent of women in India sleep less than their husbands because of housework, and many continue to work when they are ill, pregnant or in the post-partum phase. In rural areas, these effects are further exacerbated because women spend even more time fetching water and cooking food on wood or kerosene stoves. The bottom line is that to have equal homes, we need men to pitch in with housework equally or, at the very least, more than what they do currently.

I spoke with some Sikhs who embody equality in their relationships at home.

My college mate Harman Kaur is married to Inderpal Singh and they live in Gurgaon,

India. They grew up seeing their mothers do the bulk of the housework but chose differently for themselves. 'We both work full-time jobs so it only makes sense for both us to pitch in with housework,' says Kaur. 'In the first few months of marriage, I felt obliged to cook but it was honestly just a chore for me and the food I made was average at best. Inderpal actually has an interest in fresh produce and cooking techniques so now he manages dinner and we're both happier for it. I shop, supervise the cleaner and any repairs to be done at home.'

Defying traditional roles was motivated by sheer logic and practicality in their case. Harman is envied by the other women in her family for not having to enter the kitchen much but she shrugs this off. 'What does it matter if he cooks and I get the TV repaired? We're both human beings so may as well divide work based on our personalities and skillsets.'

My mother's cousin Jaspreet Singh Dhody is married to Prabhjyot, and they also thrive on a flexible system: both spouses pitch in when the cleaner takes time off or there is additional work to be done at home. They are working parents and have divided domestic chores from the beginning of their marriage. **'Words of praise and encouragement from your spouse about juggling careers, parenting and home chores go a long way in easing the burden,'** says Prabhjyot. 'Both of us openly praise each other for being supportive.'

Another friend's brother, Jasmeet Singh Hanspal, is married to India, a Sikh woman who grew up in the UK. India moved to Mumbai after marrying Jasmeet, and they live with his extended family. Both spouses work outside the home, and they have two kids. Often their weekly errands to pick up groceries become outings for the children.

Chores like laundry and dusting are a family activity. India acknowledges that the elders of the house were surprised to see their son and grandchildren doing chores and even tried to take over when her husband was doing the work. But the couple found their balance thanks to regular conversations about how to split their time during the week and even bigger discussions of what examples they'd like to set for their children. Their son now occasionally tells Jasmeet: 'Come on, Daddy, let's tidy up the room.'

Wives, mothers and mothers-in-law hovering over men doing household chores is not an uncommon trend in India. But even when men are new to doing housework, they're intelligent enough to figure things out for themselves. It was heartening to hear of older women (both Sikh and non-Sikh) who let their sons and grandsons help with household work without batting an eyelid.

My ex-colleague Romaljit Kaur Banga is married to Ranjit Singh Banga, and they have a six-year-old son. Ranjit's extended family does household chores and even helps with childcare. Both spouses work, and after office hours share the parenting load equally. Ranjit was encouraged to change diapers and feed the baby by all the women in the joint family. Another family friend, Rixi Bhatia, is married to Rajiv, who comes from a mixed-faith family. The couple lives with Rajiv's parents and Rixi's mom-in-law doesn't let her father-in-law do any domestic work. However, Rajiv and Rixi split chores and errands 50–50, and her mother-in-law encourages their partnership in household work, which makes for a compatible living situation for everyone.

Here are a few things I distilled from these conversations:

- Have empathetic conversations about what it was like growing up for both spouses, and discuss what arrangement would keep your own family happy.
- Create a system – it could be a clear division of chores or doing things jointly.
- Share the mental load, not just the physical one.
- Don't hover around them – instead, give each other frequent praise and encouragement.
- Keep it flexible – reflect and revise based on your personalities and situations.

Raising feminist kids

I'm not saying every single Sikh family practises equality within the home because that's certainly not the case. All Sikhs aren't perfectly equal in their behaviour, but perhaps they're more open to the idea because they have been taught to be so by their gurus. They practise it regularly by sitting on the floor and eating langar with everyone – no matter where they come from. When I spoke to these couples about the evolution of equality within their relationships, a common thread popped up.

Most attested that their homes and roles veered towards a more equal arrangement once they had kids. Traditional gender roles were reconfigured, and men's contribution to domestic work increased significantly once the kids came along. Perhaps, it's love for their offspring that made these fathers embrace domestic work or the fact that the entire family became cognizant of young minds watching and absorbing their parents' behaviours. Either way, I don't see anything wrong with that. Change that comes from a positive place tends to be more real and long-lasting, and setting the right example for future generations is a big part of being the change.

When Aditya and I decided to go the family way, I had a conversation with him about being an equal parent. We talked about paternity leave, fathers being caregivers and who would be taking a day off from work when the child was sick. Since the baby has arrived, he takes over in the evenings, nights as well as on weekends. As a result, I was able to write this book and get some rest and leisure time. He also weighs in on the numerous daily decisions I make as a mother, so I don't feel I am shouldering the mental load of parenthood alone.

We try to create a gender-neutral environment for our son and for our teenage nieces and nephews, whom we are very close to. Small things go a long way. My nephews see my husband set the dinner table and serve guests food and so they do the same. My nieces see me demand equality and know they can thrive in professional life and get help looking after the home. Azad will grow up seeing his father participate equally in parenting and making no bones about it.

If we want to stop perpetuating the cycle of inequality within the family, then role modelling behaviour for the next generation is key. One of my goals is to raise a feminist son, and I'm very passionate about it, so these are three things that I'm mindful of:

- **Content:** Picture books with female protagonists are a favourite in our house. Both Aditya and Azad wear plenty of pink and love playing with dolls. To learn what the older boys are consuming online, I bring up touchy topics like consent, the #MeToo movement and pornography. I ask the girls what it means to say someone is a sissy or a wuss.

- **Emotions:** I never tell my son or nephews not to cry like a girl. I tell them to cry out their feelings and that I'm there for them. To my nieces, I say tears are better out than in. A friend of mine often asks her son if he'd like to wear earrings or dresses, and even though he responds in the negative every time, she's inspired me to do the same with Azad. I want him to embrace his feminine side despite the social conditioning he will inevitably experience.

- **Roles:** Encourage the children, both girls and boys, to look after themselves but to also be caregivers for others. My cousin Gudiya Kaur Chadha assigned domestic duties to both her son and daughter during the 2020 lockdown. When her son complained about folding his sister's bra and panties as part of laundry, she explained to him that those garments were no different from male underwear. His sister was pitching in to the clean the home for the entire family, so he had to do his bit too.

A feminist tradition

My entire life I've demanded gender equality from my family. In my adolescence, I asked my family (much to their shock) why they don't make jokes about me having a boyfriend when they easily joked about my brother having a girlfriend. In my marriage, I demanded as much freedom as my husband enjoyed. When my son was born, we announced that he would have both his father's and mother's names.

I wonder sometimes whether this attitude has got to do with me being a sardarni or with me being my grandmother's granddaughter. My nani walked out of a bad marriage in 1957 and moved back into her parents' home when she was eight months pregnant. She raised my mother as a single parent at a time when there was heavy social stigma attached to being divorced. A large part of who I am is rooted in her life story, but if I take another step back, perhaps both mine and my grandmother's inner strength is tied to Sikhi.

Having grown up around relative gender equality makes us hold the world to a higher standard. Sikh first names, for instance, are gender-neutral. I once received a wedding card where the bride and groom both shared the same first name – Gurmeet. There's something powerful about this joint identity, no?

In the fifteenth century Nanak said, why condemn women, who give birth to kings and leaders? The Singh Sabha movement, which was instrumental in the revival of Sikhi in the 1870s, spoke out against ancient, sexist Indian traditions of the time such as the purdah system (which requires women to veil themselves), sati (the practice of widows jumping into their husbands' funeral pyres to end their own lives), ill treatment of widows, the practice of dowry and extravagant expenditure during marriage celebrations (the financial burden of which falls on the bride's family for the most part).

'Guru Gobind Singh was an early feminist, so when he created the Khalsa order, women and men were given the same names with the additions of Singh and Kaur,' explains Tavleen Singh. 'Even in my own childhood, I never thought of myself as lesser than my brother. My formidable grandmother was 5 foot 8 eight inches – a proper Jatt Sikh woman – and she made no distinction between my two sisters, me and my brother. All four of us were told that we have to be very brave and strong. In fact, one of my sisters used to beat our brother (and our other male cousins) to a pulp. The notion of sardarnis being strong comes from the lineage of Sikh women being prepared for battle since the days of Guru Gobind Singh.'

My last word on practising equality is a little anecdote from my wedding. During the gurdwara ceremony, an elderly aunt positioned herself behind me and insisted on patting my back to signal every time we had to stand up and sit back down. As part of Sikh wedding rituals, the bride and groom perform laavan pheras – walking in circles around the holy book – and melodious hymns are sung by priests. On one of the laavan pheras, I accidentally walked ahead of my husband and she jerked me back because tradition demands that the groom walk ahead of the bride. Then the granthi (or priest) officiating the wedding reprimanded her to say Aditya and I were equal in the eyes of God and that she needn't help us in the simple act of getting up and sitting down. He insisted that it wasn't wrong of me to have walked ahead. And all our friends and families at the ceremony could see the twinkle in my eye as we walked around for the last time, me leading the way.

The Multicultural Sikh

Colonel Manjeet Singh from the Indian army grew up seeing his father, Commander Niranjan Singh, participate equally in chores around the house. This had a remarkable impact on how their entire family embraces gender and ethnic equality. He and his four brothers are married to Sikh, Assamese-Sikh,

Catholic and Parsi women and have offspring who belong to many cultures and religious affiliations. This Sikh family effortlessly translated gender equality within the home to embracing religious diversity in their life choices – much like Sikhs do while sitting down to eat langar. I spoke with him on being married to his wife, June Mendes, a Catholic, and about how they practise equality within their family.

Q: Did your parents object to interfaith marriages?

My father was the founding president of two gurdwaras in Goa, but he had no qualms about his sons marrying women from other religions. He set an example of equality in our house by helping my mother with chores and being a very equal parent to four sons. When she was packing our tiffins in the morning, he was polishing our school shoes.

When we first told him that my younger

brother wanted to marry Roxanne Dalal, a Parsi from Bombay, he took to her and was amenable to the idea. My mother was a bit apprehensive, but he simply said, if you raise your children in cosmopolitan places like Mumbai and Goa, then you must give them the liberty of choosing their own life partners.

Q: How do you navigate the difficult moments in your marriage to a Catholic?

My wife and I stay away from aggressive religious debates but have embraced each other's cultures fully. I grew up in Goa, so I know Konkani culture and language quite well, I can sing all the folk songs and hymns. My wife wears traditional kurtas to the gurdwara and loves Punjabi food. Our two sons, Gurkirat and Simray, are Sikh and our daughter, Penny, is Catholic. Inside their hearts, they're both, I'd say. My nephew is a Sikh with Assamese features. Respecting all religions, cultures and genders is a long-standing tradition in our family.

Q: Have you ever felt societal pressure because of your unusually diverse family?

I've had extended family taunt me with the moniker Christian Sikh but I say to them: what matters is that I am Sikh. I've been through cross-border firing, fields full of landmines and life-threatening situations and come out alive because of my faith. My first posting was in Pamalpur, and the very first time I was asked to do aarti (a prayer ritual), it was noted in my record that a Sikh man did Hindu aarti singing a Christian hymn because that was the only one I knew back then!

I live life based on the teachings of our Sikh gurus. Guru Gobind Singh ji told the world: 'Manas ki jat sab ek pehchano.' This translates to recognizing all of mankind as a single caste of humanity. For me that means practising equality in my home. Even in the Japji Sahib prayer, Nanak has said: Accept all humans as your equals and let them be your only sect.

Rule # 7

Work Harder Than You Pray

One of Nanak's three core tenets is kirat karo, i.e., work hard and make an honest living. Curious to see if contemporary sardars and sardarnis are particularly hard-working and sincere, I conducted a little experiment. I sent out a WhatsApp message to about 25 friends and colleagues, asking if they could point me to examples of especially hard-working Sikhs whom they personally knew or had heard about. I often ask for such recommendations for work; I'll conduct informal polls to source interview candidates and travel recommendations through my network. Compared to all those previous times, the response to my hard-working Sikhs request was overwhelming.

Profiles of ordinary Sikhs excelling in their fields and well-known ones inspiring people of all faiths came pouring in (think Rupinder Singh Sodhi, CEO of Amul, but also my friend Surinder Singh Kainth, a global supply chain specialist at Pratt & Whitney, Connecticut). In truth, I was both surprised and not surprised. Surprised that other people remembered Sikhs beyond the conspicuous turban and Santa–Banta jokes. Not surprised because **while all Indian parents may tell their children to work hard and succeed, Sikhs have been instructed to do so by their religion.**

In the fifteenth and sixteenth centuries, Nanak sought an alternative path because he took issue with the caste system and monarchy as they were based on birth and hierarchy and not on any demonstrable quality. At the first Sikh centre in Kartarpur, everyone in the community had to till their land and work for a living, and Nanak set the example by doing so himself.

Even when the time came to choose a

successor, instead of picking one of his own sons, he selected his most worthy follower, Bhai Lehna, whom he rechristened Guru Angad (meaning 'part of my body'). This was an unusual move and even created some unrest within the community. But by sticking to his core teachings of hard work and proven skill, Nanak set an example that sardars and sardarnis have taken to heart.

In the Sikh faith, devotees are not encouraged to negotiate with God to get what they want – they're told to simply work hard. Sikhs don't fast for days or crawl at shrines or beg for forgiveness, neither from human gurus nor from the divine presence, because they've been shown the way – to simply work hard. They don't believe in superstition or wait for auspicious dates – the day they work hard is auspicious enough.

Even when something goes wrong, they don't adopt a victim mentality; instead, they go right back to work. A particularly poignant story I was pointed to was that of a Canadian Sikh doctor, Sandeep Singh Saluja. An observing Sikh, Saluja always wore a turban and kept a beard. But in the early stages of the Covid-19 pandemic, he took the difficult decision of shaving his beard so he could wear the N-95 mask properly and continue to see patients. His neighbourhood was badly hit by the virus, and Saluja considered fighting at the front lines of the pandemic his duty, both as a doctor and as a Sikh.

Punjab, where most of India's Sikhs are concentrated, saw immense prosperity in the wake of Independence. With its fertile soil and a solid irrigation system, Punjab led the Green Revolution in the country, and became a model for other Indian states to become self-sufficient. Sikhs were able to verify Nanak's tenet of kirat karo (work hard) because they had seen how working hard in the fields can lead to economic security and a good life.

They've even migrated to far-off lands like California, Vancouver and Melbourne to fill labour gaps and do the hard work that the locals shy away from. They've rebuilt lives, created communities and done well for themselves globally and are known to be one of the most successful expat communities in the world. To earn one's living through ethical means was a big part of Guru Nanak's message, so Sikhs, in addition to working hard, are also expected to be honest in their business dealings and professional lives.

This work ethic shapes their personalities and philosophies as well. We believe hard and honest work bears fruit, so we apply this learning to all aspects of our lives. We get off our butt and do immense seva for others. Both working hard at our jobs and doing seva for others come as second nature to Sikhs. For me, these two things have a strong emotional connection too. Seva benefits both the person being served and the Sikh doing the seva and further reinforces the power of working by hand. The glow or warmth I've experienced while doing selfless service is similar to being in a state of flow while writing well.

This practice of working hard helps sardars and sardarnis swing into action on many fronts. Instead of waiting for life to happen to us, we know that working at things pays dividends. So we are able to shake off inertia and obstacles and thus embrace joy, summon courage and bounce back from adversity, etc. Even though these things aren't always easy, we know working hard at imbibing them will pay off. Being sincere in business and work also helps us look at the world and our inner lives through a filter of honesty. The value of kirat karo is part of the reason why my friend Karishma was open about the pain of her mother's illness, how Nimrat Kaur embraced joy and what helped me get back to writing this book after losing my notes.

Ethics and energy management

I had a wonderful conversation with Amanpreet Singh Bajaj, General Manager, India, Southeast Asia, Hong Kong and

Taiwan, Airbnb, about energy management, productivity hacks and how his work ethic stems from the idea of honest dealings in Sikhi.

Q: Do you think Sikhi encourages hard work?

A: I'm a practising Sikh, and my religion is a big part of my life. From what wisdom my elders have transferred to me I know truthful living and a sincere attitude are emphasized in our culture. **There is a very clear expectation from all Sikhs to earn their living through labour.** The way this manifests in my life is that I keep track of my day-to-day choices that shape my long-term values. The choices we make on an hourly basis and weekly basis all add up to become our lives. When you look at it that way, there is no escaping hard work.

Q: What hacks help you be especially productive?

A: The trump hack for me has been to get to the important things first. So I always start my day with the most critical task I might have. I also believe if you're able to give the toughest assignment your best level of focus and energy, then you'll be effective at your job. Also, you won't be putting off doing something that's important. I've toyed with both methods, doing the hardest thing first and doing the easiest thing first to gain momentum. What I have found is that to tackle the hardest thing first is what works for me.

Another hack I haven't yet incorporated but really want to do is to wake up during the early hours, which are called amrit vela in Sikhi. Every time I've woken up early and had an hour to myself first thing in the morning, the results have been magical. My mind is free, nobody else is up and about, my child is still asleep, so I can set my intention for the day. It could be work or personal introspection or just being with myself, whatever will centre me. Our Guru Granth Sahib advocates waking up early because the aura around that time is positive. It can help you detach even in the face of pressing deadlines which cause stress.

Q: Do you think rest or leisure play a role in hard work?

A: In today's ever-connected world, the lines between living and working are getting blurred. I draw from the Sikh values of working for my living but also of living a family life to help bring in balance. Earlier, I found this difficult. I'd see an empty block of four hours and I'd say I can finish writing that email or complete that memo. Over the last few years, drawing a strict line and not attending meetings beyond a certain time during the day has helped me find happiness. In fact, even at work, it helps me be more productive and filter what is most important and what is not important.

How I execute this is by using my calendar a lot more. You know your deadlines, so the moment you assign time for the required work on the calendar, it clears up mind space. When you're not constantly thinking about what all you have to do, it frees up time to think more creatively and get better at problem-solving. At the end of the day, more than time management, we are in the process of energy management. The more we conserve our energy, the more we can use it for things that matter to us. At the same time, we must know that technological tools help us but they're at our disposal and we can't be at the mercy of them. It's taken time, believe me, to get here.

Fixed vs growth mindset

Nanak's understanding in the fifteenth century of living in this world and working hard is very much backed by modern science. For decades, social scientists and psychologists have been screaming from the rooftops about the power of working hard. Our tendency is to look at highly successful entrepreneurs, path-breaking academics, lauded sportsmen and award-winning actors and think of them as highly talented or good-looking or intelligent. But if one were to ask them about their journeys to success (and many researchers have), they'll confirm that sheer hard work is far more crucial to success than your natural skill, IQ or luck.

Actor Will Smith sheds wisdom on this idea. 'The only thing that I see that is distinctly different about me is I'm not afraid to die on a treadmill,' he says. 'I will not be out-worked, period. You might have more talent than me, you might be smarter than me, you might be sexier than me, you might be all of those things, you got me in nine categories. But if we get on the treadmill together, there's two things: you're getting off first, or I'm going to die. It's really that simple, right? You're not going to out-work me. It's such a simple, basic concept. The guy who is willing to hustle the most is going to be the guy that just gets that loose ball.'

In an experiment led by Hans Schroder of the University of Michigan, participants were divided into two groups and given increasingly difficult tasks. The group that was praised for their effort ('You worked really hard!') fared better after their mistakes as compared to the group that was lauded for their intellect ('You're so smart!').

Studies prove that those children who are praised for their talent develop a fixed mindset where they believe that their level of intelligence is a permanent trait and cannot be grown. Conversely, those children who are applauded for their efforts develop a growth mindset where they believe their talents can be grown through good training, hard work and persistence.

Growth mindset is another term for being resilient. It's hard not to take things personally when you're putting in serious efforts, whether it's work or personal life. Nobody becomes an expert in their field without making mistakes and persevering on in the face of them. Similarly, breaking old habits and inculcating values like gratitude, courage and resilience are rarely smooth. **Sikhs continue to work hard at both work and life because it is a core message of Nanak and, over the centuries, the idea of putting in labour to bear fruit has become a big part of the community's values.** Putting in sincere, hard work in our professional lives makes us believe in action-oriented solutions for the other aspects of life where we may struggle.

My own personal journey is no different. My father is a devout Sikh and also the strongest influence in my life. His advice to me with regard to my education and career has always been: 'Put your head down and work.' Persevere at your job despite setbacks, enjoy what you do and don't complain about long hours of work. Having this deceptively simple idea inculcated in my value system from a young age ensured that I was committed to relearning when I didn't get things right. But it wasn't necessarily a smooth ride.

At my first gig at a fashion magazine, I sucked at writing, proofreading and editing (pretty much all aspects of my job). Although I felt like a colossal failure and was tempted many times to quit, the Sikh inside me persevered on. Instead of giving up, I hustled hard, found another gig at a travel magazine and kept writing.

In a textbook case of growth mindset, I knew that I lacked skill but was passionate enough about the subject to believe that I could get better. Through the pages marked in red ink and the published stories that I knew could read more powerfully, I plugged away. Heeding the advice of my father and imbibing the culture of my community, I wrote and rewrote, thirsting for more opportunities to be bad until I got good. I approached my work from a place of humility and a complete lack of entitlement; I slowly earned my place as the favourite employee of my immediate supervisor and higher-level bosses wherever I worked.

When I grew older and more so recently, after having a baby in the midst of the pandemic, the habit of working hard has served me well. I was able to ride out tough moments and phases by swinging into action, just as my faith has taught me to do. Even if I had a bleak day or felt mentally wiped out, I persevered on because I have seen hard work pay off in my professional life. It helped me have faith in my own ability to make my life and situation better, and eventually things did look up.

Let's break down the idea of working hard, so we can implement it practically.

The 10k rule

Psychologists Benjamin Bloom and K. Anders Ericsson have even been able to quantify the amount of work required to become an expert in your field. According to them, whether you want to master pottery, accounting or swimming, you need ten thousand hours of practice to accomplish that goal.

I first read about the 10k rule in Malcom Gladwell's book *Outliers*, which has an early chapter full of fascinating stories of icons like The Beatles and Bill Gates practising their skill for at least 10,000 hours before becoming successful. It was also noted that this 10k figure typically takes ten years to complete.

I read this research at the beginning of my journalistic career in 2010, and somehow the figure stuck with me. But at no point has it resonated as strongly as in 2021 – approximately ten years later. A decade of writing travel and lifestyle articles has given me the ability to produce them almost with my eyes closed, without compromising on quality. I recently got the biggest compliment of my career on a story I'd written while on vacation in Goa, hungover and racing to catch a flight. I am living proof that practice makes perfect and that there is no shortcut to the 10k rule.

So if grit matters more than talent, how does one actually get to that figure of 10,000 hours? Juggling between a baby and a book forced me to rethink my productivity strategy and I came up with a few hacks. I also spoke with numerous Sikhs I discovered through my WhatsApp poll about their real-life hacks for working hard in professions and businesses.

Single tasking

I started work on this book when my baby was five weeks old and working with a newborn certainly came with a set of challenges. I was far more scattered and in the beginning, I ran out if I heard Azad cry even a little. It was evident that my working style and space were going to need an upgrade. Even otherwise, many of us are stuck to methods and routines established at the beginning of our careers. Meanwhile, science, technology and the wellness fields have made incredible discoveries about how people can work not just better but also smarter. Why not arm ourselves with this knowledge?

To avoid jumping up every time Azad yelped and then losing focus when I returned to the desk, I decided on two big changes in my work life: first, I moved to a distraction-free workspace and, second, I stopped multitasking and did one thing at a time. Since renting a desk at a co-working space was not an option during the pandemic, I left my baby with my husband, who was working from home, and went to my parents' home to work quite often. Even while I was there I left my smartphone in another room and only checked it once I was done with a particular task. This was a game-changer and helped me accomplish a lot in a few hours. When you know you don't have time to procrastinate your productivity can leap.

Once I was set up and ready to work, I switched to doing one thing at a time. As part of my research for the book I read that multitasking is not helpful to productivity but is in fact the opposite – studies show it hampers accuracy and efficiency and reduces overall cognitive performance. My frenetic mental pace as a new mother was making it hard to focus so single tasking went a long way in helping me take a breath, get started and finish something instead of nothing. Switching to single tasking was not easy but my old habit of writing things down helped me implement it.

Note taking

As an intern at a newspaper, I set out to cover a press conference by myself and my boss told me, 'Just write every single thing down and then we'll make sense of it when you get back'. It was great advice. I've been a notorious note taker since then. In my student life, it helped me remember my lessons and get better grades. Through my journalism career, writing things down helped retain the finer details of travel that get lost in fleeting memory. I find that thorough note taking also help me focus on the relevant information, makes me a better interviewer and helps me listen better.

The reason I'd been so upset over my lost notes is that I had made scores of strong connections between texts and my own ideas while I was handwriting those notes down. So in the wake of having a baby, I went to this practice with a vengeance. I made notes in the margins of the books that I read as research. Every morning, I wrote down in a notebook the three tasks I needed to complete (this helped me focus on a limited number of daily goals). I kept a notebook near me all day, so every time I had a sudden brainwave for another chapter or baby-related query, I quickly noted it down and continued on with my current task, instead of interrupting my flow. I recommend it to everyone not just writers.

Work smart – not just hard

Exactly how much work does one need to do to qualify as a hard-working individual?

To answer this question, I divided the 10k figure into a regular work week, and the answer was 20 hours a week. For people working 50 to 60 hours in the office, this seems paltry, but here's the catch. Those 20 hours have to be spent on the specific skill you're trying to improve, and you have to challenge yourself to work one level above your current skill. It's crucial to honestly gauge whether you are doing this or not. For instance, when I switched from fashion to travel writing, I first aced writing bite sized copy, then short articles, then I mastered the monthly five-page shopping story and eventually the meaty ten-page feature. My time spent sitting in meetings, answering emails, looking over proofs, doing other research were aside from those 20 hours a week I spent specifically improving my writing skills.

Psychologist and author Angela Duckworth has termed this 'deliberate practice' in her book Grit: *Why Passion and Resilience Are the Secrets to Success*. She also quotes K. Anders Ericsson's 10,000-hour rule but goes a bit deeper into the idea. 'This is how experts practice,' she writes. 'First they set a "stretch goal", zeroing in on just one narrow aspect of their overall performance. Rather than focus on what they already do well, experts strive to improve specific weaknesses. They intentionally seek out challenges they can't yet meet . . . Then, with undivided attention and great effort, experts strive to reach their stretch goal. Interestingly, many choose to do so while nobody's watching.'

No wonder we all want to believe in genius! We don't usually get to see the hard work that goes behind world-famous achievements. I spoke with another sardarni who used her decade in event management to slowly up her skill set and get where she wanted to be. Supreet Kaur was hired by event management firm OML in 2011. In the beginning, her responsibility was to manage artists, but what she really wanted was a piece of the firm's largest property – the NH7 music festival. The first opportunity she got to work with NH7 was to be part of the technical requirements team. She knew nothing about music equipment but spent that year reading manuals, doing online research and calling vendors to learn the micro details. The next year, she headed the technical team, and by 2019, Supreet Kaur was Festival Director of NH7. Her deliberate practice had paid off, and she had become an expert in creating largescale experiences for music lovers.

I also spoke with my uncle Harjeet Singh Rekhi, who grew up in a Sikh household where working hard and becoming financially independent was given importance. He's worked in marketing since the 1980s and was invited to shift base from New Delhi to Singapore because of his uber-successful campaigns that drove sales until stocks sold out. Currently he's the Global Head of Digital Cities for Dell Technologies and attributes his quick rise through the ranks to effective time management. If time management sounds too basic to be a game-changing skill, think about any office you've worked in and you'll be able to point out the employees or entrepreneurs who managed their time effectively and those who straggled until the end of the day to finish daily tasks.

Every Sunday evening, Rekhi reviews his coming week to mentally prepare and also sends out requests for all the data and information that he may need from other colleagues. Rekhi has another neat trick where he works backwards from his day of presentation and schedules what needs to be done the day prior, week prior and sometimes month prior too. 'Only if I prep correctly for all the foreseeable issues will I have bandwidth to deal with the unforeseeable challenges,' he adds. Effective time management helps him avoid last-minute panic and impress his bosses by having answers to tough questions.

Cultivate your EQ (along with your IQ)

Kaur's thirst for excellence and Rekhi's discipline of time management made me wonder what set them apart. I dug deeper and came to the conclusion is that they're individuals who are navigating their professional lives with awareness. Having good EQ is key to many soft skills like taking feedback well, making clear decisions, taking ownership of our mistakes, being a team player, respecting other people's time, stress management and so on. People who pay attention to their personal growth flourish as employees, colleagues, peers and bosses.

So how do we use our emotional intelligence to work better?

1. The first step is always awareness. Pay attention to what you are feeling on a normal day versus when something positive or negative happens at work. Observe if there is a difference in your communication with colleagues based on your emotions. Don't make decisions until you cool down.

2. Manage your stress, whether you do it by cracking jokes like my father or through physical exercise or waking up early for some me-time as Bajaj suggested.

3. 'It's important to practice listening with intention,' says Kaur. 'When you really listen and pay attention to nonverbal cues, you can ask quality questions and learn to take feedback. This manifests into leadership growth mentality eventually.'

4. Be more empathic. Analyze how you respond when you disagree with a colleague. Do you hear them out even if you think they're wrong? Do you acknowledge the emotion behind their point of view?

5. Remember, however it may look from the outside, nobody likes all the tasks associated with their jobs but they do them anyway. I was a travel writer but I spent a lot of my time at the desk interviewing local insider's about their favourite spots and creating rich stories from internet research. My solution to this was to get better at my job until my supervisor started recommending my name for the travel gigs.

Ride the passion high

A few hard-working Sikhs I spoke to fell into the category of wildly creative folks who worked on the field under demanding conditions and crazy long hours. Tejinder Singh Khamkha is a photographer on Bollywood movie sets – an environment known to be especially gruelling, with workdays that occasionally stretch to 36, 48 or 72 hours! He attributes his drive for getting through crazy movie schedules to his fiery passion and his experiencing a 'high' while doing his job. However, for many years his parents were not sure he'd chosen the right path by opting to be a photographer over a traditionally lucrative profession.

Many young people looking to pursue off-beat careers don't find the familial support they need. Often parents want to see financial stability in their children's futures more than anything else, and their children grow up hearing this message. But consider this: a study by Gallup says that 85 per cent of employees worldwide are not engaged in the workplace in 2021. This is huge because, according to science, not only do we perform better at work when we are interested in it but we are happier when we spend our lives doing something we like (sounds like common sense but it isn't commonly practiced).

So how is it that some of us find our passions early in life, while a vast majority are not working in fields they have an interest in? Duckworth addresses passion in her book and advises people to explore sufficiently early in their careers. Finding your passion can be a confusing journey and one that requires you and your family to have patience. She points out that we assume passion should hit us like a bolt of lightning, but in reality it can involve going down wrong paths and engaging with your passion long enough to learn its nuances before you make it your life's calling. I am aware that, for many, class and financial situations create insurmountable hurdles in the path of pursuing their passion. But when you do have the choice, choosing your passion over the more practical or easier option will ensure that you'll be good at what you do and be happier too. Perhaps then hard work won't feel so hard.

Live in Chardi Kala

Rajinder Singh Harzall is a British Sikh born in the year of India's independence. His father, Corporal Makhan Singh, fought in the Second World War as part of the British Indian army and he introduced six-year-old Harzall to skipping. It was a way to stay occupied and keep negative thoughts at bay. Harzall stayed active throughout his life and eats healthy, simple food like bread and butter with turmeric.

His daily routine includes waking up at 4 a.m. to pray, followed by a trip to the gurdwara. He spends his days doing seva, first a skipping challenge with Khalsa primary schoolkids in Slough and then he takes cake and food to homeless shelters. Almost seventy-five years old, he continues to skip, runs marathons for charity and combines his love for exercise with the tradition of selfless service encouraged by his faith.

When London's lockdown hit, Harzall's daughter Minreet was worried about how her parents would cope being stuck inside the house, unable to meet their community or visit the gurdwara. She suggested that her father start a skipping challenge on YouTube to help other people stay active during the lockdown. In typical Sikh fashion, Minreet's answer to help her family included helping strangers too. She uploaded the first skipping video and, to her surprise, it went viral.

Harzall's skipping challenge has been covered by CNN, BBC and major Indian news media since then. At the time of our conversation, Harzall had raised over £14,000 for the UK's National Health Service and was awarded the Points of Light honour by Prime Minister Boris Johnson.

He seemed unaffected by all the attention

his videos attracted. 'If I can give back and help people, it makes my cause worthwhile,' he said. 'Fame doesn't matter. I'm happy to help people learn how to skip and stay active. My body is my temple, and exercising makes me feel happy, alert and energetic. It helps me be in chardi kala every day of my life.'

Harzall wasn't the first person to mention chardi kala to me. Through my journey of writing this book, as I spoke to Sikhs from around the world, the words chardi kala kept coming up. We'd be talking about humour or courage or hard work, but **chardi kala emerged as the spirit that makes Sikhs who they are**. And that is why I decided to end this book with a chapter dedicated to these two words.

What is chardi kala?

The words chardi kala are part of the refrain which ends the Sikh ardaas, recited daily in the gurdwara and on all important occasions in

Sikh homes. I translated it in my introduction, but it bears repeating here:

Nanak naam chardi kala, tere bhane sarbat da bhala

(Nanak, with naam, that is, divinity, comes eternal positivity. With God's will, may there be peace and prosperity for everyone in the world)

Chardi kala literally means eternal positivity, but people also interpret it as a buoyant attitude to life, being in high spirits or channelling optimism in both happy and troubled times. Sikh gurus have explicitly told their followers to say the words when life deals them a blow, so sardars and sardarnis know what to fall back on when adversity hits.

Chardi kala is what inspires Sikhs to enjoy life and laugh easily. It's what helps us build resilience and develop a growth mindset. It's why Hasmeet Singh Chandok created the bhangra

YouTube videos and why the protesting farmers fed the policemen. It's why Nimrat cooks, cleans and dances daily and why Manjeet Singh and his family embrace diversity. It's why my father makes everyone around him chuckle and why my nani and her generation are not embittered from the traumas of Partition and 1984.

The ultimate secret of Sikhs doing good is that they do it from a place of enjoyment, of pleasure, laughter and companionship. Being good isn't drudgery for us. On the contrary, it's a joy, and that's why the community does it over and over again, bigger and better each time. We all know how to be good, or to do right. But it feels difficult. Sikhi's transformative idea is to turn doing good into a celebration.

Just as Buddhism has mindfulness, Taoism has contentment, Danish culture has hygge (cosiness), Sikhi has chardi kala. What makes Sikhi different is that it's not focused on reaching a happy place, but on manifesting happiness in every place, using a positive attitude to approach life with hard work, benevolence, service and joy.

To live in chardi kala means to break the habit of complaining and to try to look for a silver lining. If you've lost your job, look at it as an opportunity to evaluate your life's purpose or spend time with your kids. I know of people who managed the stress of catching the coronavirus by thinking of future travel once the antibodies kicked in. If that's too much, start by reframing a relatively minor stress. You don't even need to be religious to adopt this logic. Author and business consultant Harrison Owen has written these Four Immutable Laws of the Spirit:

i.   Whoever is present are the right people.

ii. Whenever it begins is the right time.

iii. Whatever happens is the only thing that could have happened.

iv. And when it's over, it's over.

The mindful chef

I'm surrounded by Sikhs, and so can observe how they're able to live in chardi kala. I spoke with celebrity chef Ranveer Brar, a truly wise soul who makes mindfulness accessible to everyone through his simple yet insightful words.

Q: Where did you first hear the words chardi kala?
Brar: All Sikh children grow up with the refrain 'Nanak naam chardi kala, tere bhane sarbat da bhala' in their gurdwara or home. When we hear those words, everyone knows it's the end of the ardaas and time to bow down to the Guru Granth Sahib in surrender. As a child, the words chardi kala were my signal to physically bow (I didn't want to risk embarrassment by leaning down at the wrong time), but I never really contemplated the meaning of those words until I got much older.

Q: What does chardi kala mean to you?

Brar: For me there are two meaningful concepts in this refrain. The first is bhana or God's will. Things will happen beyond your control, so we have to learn to accept them for what they are. They say, 'tera bhana meetha laage', which means you've got to find sweetness in God's will even if it is not how you'd like it to be. It seems distressing, ugly or bad, but only gradually do you realize that the line means a lot. It probably means everything. People have so many interpretations for chardi kala, but to me it means equanimity of the mind.

Q: Any particular time in life when being in chardi kala really helped you?

Brar: When I lived in New York, I went through a tough phase and had to close the doors to my Indo-French restaurant, Banq. It became very heartbreaking towards the end.

I had never seen failure before because I was a very successful chef in India. I moved to Boston after that and really went back to the gurdwara to try to find answers within my upbringing and my religion. I started doing seva and making langar – something I'd done for a large part of my childhood. That's when I learnt to surrender to God's will and realized that as long as I have the right state of mind, all will be well.

I always say there's the religion you were born with and the religion you mindfully adopt. In India, you're not usually given a choice because you're born into it. For me, I adopted Sikhi in the true sense at that time. I got to test it out and saw it works for me. Chardi kala helps me stay uplifted during my troubles but it also continues in good times because I remember that tranquil state of mind and tune back to it.

The pessimist takes a personality test

While researching for this book, I read *Learned Optimism*, by Martin Seligman, who is the father of happiness research in contemporary psychology. Something happened that left me (in Gen Z language) shook. Early in the book, there's a quiz to ascertain how optimistic you are. I haven't taken a personality quiz since I was 20, so I took it on as a fun exercise. When I scored myself, I got the highest possible rating, which meant that I am wildly optimistic.

Let me explain why this result caught me so off guard. I've explained in my introduction that the community as a whole imbibes certain values but not every Sikh is brave and generous and resilient and funny and hard-working. I am a classic example of a Sikh who has often struggled with a positive outlook. I have always been a dark, temperamental writer and thought of myself as a pessimist-realist at best. I'm certain I was honest while taking the optimism test. Either it wasn't accurate (bear in mind that it was created by Seligman, not a teen-magazine writer) or my self-analysis was flawed. Either way, it did get me thinking about myself differently.

Studies show that if you act more positive, energetic and high-spirited, you become those things too. Towards the very end of this book project, I saw this thesis play out in my own behaviour. As the deadline for my manuscript submission drew nearer, I experienced a surge of positivity and felt excited, instead of stressed. Usually even when I feel positive about something, I'm embarrassed or afraid to say it aloud. This time, it was strangely different. As family and friends asked me how I felt being so close to the book's completion, I often said, 'I feel really positive and good. I'm excited to have written the book and am looking forward to it being out in the world.'

I did a two-week countdown to my submission on Instagram and was pleased to exchange motivational messages with colleagues, friends, old schoolmates and even strangers. I'd be eager to attack the pages every day, instead of feeling dread that I wouldn't succeed or that writing is painful. This helped me stay on track with my schedule and, on a couple of occasions, get ahead of it as well.

That's not to say that I didn't struggle with revision. Three days before my book submission date, my ten-month-old baby developed unexplained, high-grade fever, and I lost two days collecting urine samples, running blood tests and visiting the hospital for a chest X-ray. With the fever not responding to medicine, my husband and I spent many hours sponging him to bring it down and barely slept so as to monitor his temperature through the night.

Ordinarily, I would have adopted a negative outlook and lamented about things being especially hard at a crucial time. But this time, I stayed patient and had faith that everything would work out for the best. A day before submission, my husband's family took over, and I spent the day at my parents' home, furiously wrapping up as much as I could. The more I accomplished, the better I felt, and the better I felt, the more I was able to take things in my stride and persevere.

It seems all the conversations I'd been having with Sikhs had rubbed off on me. Hearing people's personal accounts of living life fully, doing seva and living in the spirit of chardi kala gave me confidence in the idea. Certainly it's lighter on the heart to live life expecting good outcomes than morose ones. Had writing a book about Sikhs made me more Sikh? I'm delighted to say I think so.

Summing up

In a world where one feels torn about what to feel hopeless about (from climate change to the political extremities to natural disasters, including pandemics), I want to end this book on a note of hope. Guru Nanak took a radical yet humble idea of selfless service and transformed an entire community through it. Each sardar and sardarni is only a drop in the sea, but look at what the collective ocean of Sikhi puts forth into the world.

All the things we've discussed in this book about Sikh values and culture play into this trait of doing good. Sikhs do good not because of a singular trait, but because the seven qualities of hard work, service, joy, laughter, resilience, courage and equality often flow into each other. When you come from a happy, ethical, strong place, doing more good becomes a joyful act and not burdensome at all.

We do seva regularly in gurdwara kitchens, medical camps and disaster zones because Guru Nanak told us seva is as important as prayer. Helping those less privileged than you directs your thoughts from your personal worries to others' misfortunes and also brings gratitude for your own life. Sikhs cook langars, clean mosques and rebuild homes in a meditative rhythm to convert inner anxiety into actions that benefit others. Working with your hands was Nanak's strategy of setting in motion an endless chain of positivity, appreciation and resilience in the real world.

We don't shy away from chasing happiness and enjoy pleasures guilt-free. But we also know how to bring joy into daily life – by eating together, cracking jokes, spending time with loved ones and singing and dancing with gusto. Singhs and Kaurs have been instructed by their religion to find their miri piri, the balance between materialistic happiness and spiritual joy. Our strong code of ethics helps us discard outside judgement and live fully. Living with both bursts of happiness and daily joy helps us channel mindfulness and chardi kala, irrespective of whether life gives us lemons or lemonade.

We practise equality and show dignity and respect to both men and women as well as to people from diverse faiths, castes and economic backgrounds. We go a step further and embrace them in our brotherhood by breaking bread with them on the floors of our gurdwaras. We don't need anyone to convert to our religion because our doors are open to everyone, especially in times of natural disasters and terrorist attacks. Our holiest site is called Harmandir Sahib, i.e., everyone's temple, and it has four doors in the four directions to welcome everyone looking to find peace, pray or just eat a comforting meal. Inclusivity is in our DNA, and the community and goodwill it generates celebrates the good we send out to the world – from Patiala to Paris.

We act courageously on behalf of the weak even at great personal cost. When it comes to standing up against bullies, we don't differentiate between Sikh and non-Sikh victims. Living with bravery and honour is a long-standing tradition in Sikhi, from the warriors' part of the Khalsa order created by Guru Gobind Singh to Maharaja Ranjit Singh's martial experts to the gallantry awards won by Sikh regiments in the Indian army. It helps us feel good about our contributions to society and even our mere existence. Again, this inner confidence shines through as positivity.

Resilience is another name for chardi kala, albeit with a connotation of bouncing back from adversity. Sikhs have the ability to rise above their circumstances and do good even in adversity because we have been taught by our religion to practise gratitude. It is what keeps our spirits alive and kicking on the darkest of days when we've seen our land ripped apart and racist hate crimes are perpetrated against us. The examples that our gurus and fellow Sikhs have laid before us are our inspiration not to sink but to swim when life hits us hard.

Working hard brings meaning and purpose to our lives. One of Guru Nanak's core messages was to work hard and earn a living through honest means. Whether you're a taxi driver in New York or a tycoon in New Delhi, it's not just profits but also ethics in professional life that is emphasized in Sikhi. We Sikhs have embodied this teaching with great integrity and also seen prosperity through the fruit of our labour. We have faith in our own ability to work hard and do well for ourselves, and this gives us security and confidence. After tilling the field all day, a Sikh farmer enjoys a good meal with the family (and perhaps a peg or two) and falls back into the sweet sleep that comes after working with sincerity.

We have the ability to laugh at ourselves and make others laugh too. This is probably my favourite thing about my own community. We can take a joke because of our strength rooted in our self-worth and we can tell jokes to become endearing to outsiders. I've seen at first-hand how powerful humour can be in communication, and Sikhs know how to be funny without trying too hard. If that isn't positivity, I don't know what is.

This is what it means to live in chardi kala. We Sikhs chant these two words in every moment of our lives, on ordinary days when we visit the gurdwara, at weddings and celebrations and to each other, in conversations when morale is low. Whatever you choose to learn or not learn from this book, if I can make you hope and believe that we can help and rely on each other, that we can face adversity and still laugh, that we can live large and also be selfless, I will consider this book a worthy effort.

Acknowledgements

I was stuck home in the Covid-19 lockdown with a five-week-old baby when the Juggernaut team reached out, asking if I'd like to write a book about Sikhs. I said yes almost immediately. My publisher, Chiki Sarkar, helped me fulfil a childhood dream with this book. Chiki, thank you for believing that I could produce my first publishable manuscript in the throes of new motherhood, for holding my hand through the process and also for the kindness you've shown me along the way (that two-month sabbatical was instrumental in calming my overloaded brain).

My mentor and best friend Divia Thani is the one who recommended my name for this book (I believe her precise words were: 'She's just had a baby, but if anyone can do it, this girl can'). Divia was my boss during my five-year tenure as a magazine writer at *Condé Nast Traveller* India. She has always been incredibly generous with giving me opportunities to do great things and also with her hyperbolic praise.

The book is dedicated to my parents, but I have to mention other family members here too. My nani, who was decades ahead of her time, is my inspiration to tread my own path. My husband, Aditya, who is more Sikh than I am, is the wind beneath my wings. My brother, Shaan, is my biggest supporter. My sisters, Shivani and Sadhvi, have been my rocks ever since I got married, and my niece, Yashita, is my wisest child.

I'd also like to thank my girlfriends without whom I wouldn't be who I am. Sana Rafi is a published author herself; we met as undergraduates in rural Pennsylvania in 2002 and signed our book deals almost at the same time – the universe ensures that our lives always,

always collide. My childhood best friends Reema, Namrata, Triman, Preet and Anisha have always championed me, and it is only with their support, counsel and shoulders to cry on that I could balance raising a baby and writing a book. The Hard Core gang is gold. Sunayana, Karishma, Nitika, Mallu and Surashmi I met later in life, but they've also supported this endeavour unwaveringly.

Lastly I want to thank the invisible forces that went into the making of this book. Simone, my intern, worked incredibly hard with me on this project. She made the writing process feel less lonely by cheering and sighing with me every step of the way. Amruta is a translator and editor by profession and also a friend; she was my most valuable reader and helped bang this baby into shape. Also, my gynaecologist and friend Dr Munjaal V. Kapadia, for taking such good care of me and my family during the pandemic and answering my calls at all hours of the day.

To the universe: thank you for making this happen, I am grateful.